Made2Thrive

13 PROVEN PRACTICES TO HELP YOU
ON YOUR JOURNEY OF SUCCESS

TONY OJEDA

Made2Thrive is published by Integrity Center in Lincoln, Nebraska

ISBN: 978-1-7359624-0-5 (paperback)
ISBN: 978-1-7359624-1-2 (ebook)

Cover Design by 100 Covers
For more information, email thrive@made2thrive.live

Free Gift For You!!!

For a printable pdf poster of the 13 Proven Practices
to Help You on Your Journey of Success please
go to https://made2thrive.live/launch-page/

We will also give you a free coaching consultation
if you wish! This is not required to download the
printable pdf poster, but we would encourage you to
take advantage of it. This is a $350 value. We will follow
up with you after your download the poster to see if
you would like to schedule a 60 minute consultation.

Feel free to contact us with questions by
emailing us at thrive@made2thrive.live.

For my wife, Cyndi, and my children, Rachel, Andrew, Lindsay, Samuel, Emma, and Joseph. I am blessed by all of you, and you help me to thrive each day!

Contents

Success Defined And The
Four Pillars of Success

Becoming Exceptional
On Your Journey

Tools For Business And Career

Tips For Taking You To The Top

Introduction

Before you actually commit to continuing to leaf through this small book, it would be beneficial to anyone who may be reading to have a little background on the author, the one who is charging you to thrive and champion the phrase "Made To Thrive." So here is a little bit about me, my story, and why I believe we all, as human beings, are made to thrive, and why I have taken the time to write this book. I hope this will be helpful for anyone who reads it.

I have been a Financial Advisor/Insurance Agent/ Financial Counselor/Investment Guy/Financial Coach, or any other term you might want to use, for over 26 years. Throughout my career, I have been very blessed to help a number of clients achieve their financial dreams and goals. The work that I do fills me with great joy, and I get paid well for doing it. What could be better than that? Excelling and enjoying the work that you do is not always the case for everyone. Usually, it is either one or the other. You either love your job, but don't do well, or you do well, but hate your job. I have been blessed to both enjoy what I do and to be good at it.

I am not the top Producer in the country, but I am successful—more successful than most in my industry. As a result of my hard work and progress, I have been a member of the Million Dollar Round Table for almost twenty years and a member of the Court of The Table for the past 10 years. I have also been a member of the Top of The Table this past year. Twelve years ago I made about $160,000 of total revenue. In 2017 I was just over $750,000 of total revenue. I don't share this with you to brag, but just to give you some perspective of what I have accomplished. My hope in sharing this information with you is that it might at least establish some sort of credibility for me to write this book. Ultimately, this does not even define what success is. I will touch on that in a later chapter.

Over the past few years, I have been asked by many other advisors within the industry what I have done to be so successful. Heck, to some it may seem like I am an overnight success. Trust me, that isn't even close to the truth. I have worked extremely hard and wisely to become an overnight success for the past 26 years. The first 10 years of my career I worked really hard, but not very wisely. In fact, looking back I would say that I worked pretty foolishly, and made many mistakes. I wish I would have been much more intentional about "working smart" when I first started my career. Unfortunately, that was not the case.

I have already shared with you that in 2017 I made just over $750,000 in total revenue. Very recently I did leave my former firm, sold my stock, and purchased back some of my book of business. I would suspect that moving forward I could expect total revenue of about $500,000, and even though that is less than I had in revenue before, it is an amount that is more than sufficient to provide for my family, give us the lifestyle that we desire, as well as the ability to give a lot away to meaningful organizations that we like to support. That revenue will also be enough to allow me to save enough so I can retire by the time I am in my very early 60s. I doubt I will retire by then because I love what I do. This, however, does not change the fact that I will be financially independent when that season of life comes upon me.

What I have not shared with you yet is that I currently only work 3.5 days per week. I do not partake in the seemingly endless "grind" that others within my industry trudge through. Life was not always like that though. Let's run the clock back to early 2010. The New York Yankees had just won the Fall Classic in 2009, President Obama was beginning his second year as President, and just about everyone had Bieber Fever. Back then, I was leading our firm as Managing Partner. We had around 30 employees working for us. I worked as a Managing Partner while at the same taking care of my own book of business as a Financial Advisor. If you would have asked me ten years ago if I would ever see myself only working 3.5 days per week I would have told you that you were absolutely insane.

However, as I alluded to previously, I left that firm and sold my stock. The reason I chose to sell my stock and purchase back most of my book of business from my old firm was to allow me to have more flexibility and to be more focused on the aspect of the business I enjoyed most, meeting with my clients and helping them to achieve their life goals. It also allowed me to define what my objectives were without worrying about the objectives of others in my firm.

Each of us has a unique calling in life, a calling that is specifically made out for each one of us as individuals. It is not my intention in writing this book to tell you what your life calling is, and it is also not my intention that you would do everything that I have done. Rather, what I want readers to understand after reading this book is that each person has to find their own path, as well as figure out what steps they need to take in order to help them achieve their own personal vision. My hope is that the ideas I share may be helpful to you, to stimulate you to want to thrive in your own life.

We have so little time on earth, regardless of when our Heavenly Father decides to give us our last breath. Therefore, we should be focused every day on doing everything we can to thrive in the life that He has given us. In fact, even if one lives to be 85, that is only 31,025 days on this earth. I have already been on this earth for over 18,000 days and it has gone by very quickly. We don't have very much time while on this earth to truly make a difference, so we ought to take advantage of every opportunity we have been given.

I believe we were made to thrive, and how we do that each day is up to us. I am passionate about serving others, whether that is in my business working with my clients, giving 100% to my wife, spending time with my kids and helping them to grow, or serving my community. I believe I have unique gifts to serve others, and I believe you do as well. We were made to thrive! I look forward to traveling with you on this journey. The more we thrive in this world, the better off the world will be. There is so much good to do, and so little time to do it. Lets go!!!!

Success Defined And The Four Pillars of Success

Success

For most of my life I really did not know what success meant. I thought I did, but up until about three years ago I did not truly know what it was.

When I was in High School I ran Cross Country and Track & Field. I thought I would be a success if I became a State Champion. Everything I did in High School was pointed at trying to be a State Champion. I stayed away from partying and drugs and alcohol. I dated a couple of girls, but they were not my first loves. My first love was running and becoming a State Champion. I put in a whole lot of work to be a State Champion.

Here's the deal—I never became a State Champion. My Senior Year I finished 13th at the State Meet in Cross Country. I was a State Medalist, but I wasn't a State Champion. In Track going into the District Meet I had the fifth fastest time in the 3200 Meters for the entire state. However, a girl got in the way. Instead of focusing on my race, I stayed up late the night before the District Meet talking to her. I got a horrible night's sleep, and although I should have been District Champion in the 3200 Meters, I didn't even place or qualify for the State Meet. I definitely was not a State Champion in Track. I guess I was a total failure.

I went to Nebraska Wesleyan University, a Division III school in Lincoln, Nebraska. I ran Cross Country and Track there too for my first year and a half. In my first career collegiate Cross Country race I beat the previous year's High School Cross Country and 3200 Meter State Champion and State Runner Up. I would have been absolutely excited to ever have beaten him in high school. I worked so hard for so long to do that very thing, but never did. Now, I was not so excited. I actually did not know he was even in the race until afterward. I finished about 26th in the race, so I did not feel so successful.

I thought if I was going to be a success then I would have to be a National Champion, get done with school, become the best American runner and ultimately win a Gold Medal in the Olympics. Guess what? Yep, I didn't even get close. My freshman year at Wesleyan we went to the National Championships of Cross Country and I finished around 100th. I ended up getting misdiagnosed with a hiatal hernia my sophomore year, and my hopes and dreams of being a success were over.

I became a Financial Advisor in June 1994 and began setting goals to be a success. I wanted to be the top producer in my agency. In fact, I wanted to be the top producer for the entire company. Surely, if I worked hard enough, I would become a success. So, I worked and worked and worked, and guess what? Nope, I never was the top producer in that agency. My Dad was several times, but not me. Once again, I guess I was just a miserable failure.

No matter how hard I worked, working 60 hours plus per week, no matter how many people I tried to meet with I just could not get to the top. Same as when I was in high school and college. No matter how hard I worked and how many miles I ran I just couldn't get to the very top of the running world. How in the world can anyone be successful in their sport, business, or call if only one person can be at the very top?

Selling my stock at my old firm and starting my own firm allowed me to be more successful. Success is not defined by how much money we make or how many accounts we open. I see success as our ability to do what we want to do in life while at the same time helping as many other people as possible to do what they want in life.

Earl Nightingale, the great personal productivity speaker and author, defined success as "the progressive realization of a worthy idea."[1] Notice that he does not say the completion of the worthy idea. What he means is that success is really all about the journey we take rather than the achievement of the goal. It doesn't mean that you have finally arrived, but more that you are arriving. It is not about the final destination, but about the journey to that destination. It is not about accomplishing your goals or vision, but about the action steps you take to achieve your goals and vision. We have a life vision. We are not successful if we achieve it, but we are successful if we are moving toward our vision every day. If we are not moving toward

---

[1] "Success: a worthy destination Nightingale-Conant." http://www.nightingale.com/articles/success-a-worthy-destination/.

our objective every day and we are just resting on our laurels, then we are not a success.

John Maxwell, a leading expert on leadership and personal development says, "Another common misconception is that people have achieved success when they feel successful or happy."[2] He also suggests that some people feel that success means possessing things. In addition, many people define success as having achieved something, but that is not success. Success is knowing your purpose in life, growing to reach your maximum potential, and sowing seeds that benefit others."[3] It is an ongoing journey, he says. Maxwell affirms the theme of Nightingale. It is the journey, and more specifically it is the journey of not only growing to achieve your potential and goals, but also helping others. Success is not a destination, otherwise when you reach the destination there is nothing else to go for. We continue to grow each day and we are never finished growing until God Himself takes us from this earth.

We were made to thrive, and we should strive to thrive each day. Hoping for a good future without investing in today is a surefire way to not be successful. That would be like a farmer waiting for a crop without ever planting any seed. Maxwell says, "The secret of your success is determined by your daily agenda... Successful people make right decisions early and manage those decisions daily."[4] The journey in life is not a sprint. It is truly a marathon. Actually

[2]   John Maxwell, *3 Things Successful People Do*, (Nashville: Nelson Books, 2016), p. 9.

[3]   *Ibid.*, p. 11.

[4]   John Maxwell, *Today Matters* (New York: Time Warner Book Group, 2004), pp. 14-15.

a better analogy may be that the journey is much more like an ultra-marathon. It goes on and on and on. Each day we have to work on it. We must have things laid out each day based upon those things that are most important to us. We then need to take action to get closer to our destination.

Maxwell is a big believer in being very intentional with each and every day. He believes that you cannot just leave how a day unfolds to chance. If you do that then you will not be successful. He asks, "What's the key to a life that matters? Living each day with intentionality... When you intentionally use your everyday life to bring about positive change in the lives of others, you begin to live a life that matters."[5] The emphasis here by Maxwell is twofold. The first is to be very intentional and the second is to have a positive impact on others. Maxwell believes success needs both of these aspects. If you are all about yourself and con- sumed with you then you cannot be successful. You cannot thrive unless you are having a significant impact on others.

I own a beautiful wood carving made by Christians in the Holy Land. They would come to my church once a year with all of their hand-made carvings, icons, rosaries, and other religious goods. This particular carving is an image of Jesus washing the feet of Peter. I have it on my desk to remind me daily that I need to serve others. If I just serve myself then I am not a person who is going to thrive.

Ultimately it comes down to our attitude. If we have a down and negative attitude there is no way in the world we can become successful. We have to believe that we can be

---

[5] John Maxwell, *Intentional Living*, (New York: Hachette Book Group, 2017), p. 4.

successful and that the actions we take daily will lead us in the right direction. I try very hard to have a positive attitude each day. Sometimes, though, things just go wrong, and it seems like a day can start spiraling out of control. This can lead me to be negative and also lead to negative self-talk. I then think to myself that being negative is not going to help me achieve my objectives, and I find some way to stay positive. It might be that I just step away from my desk or office for a bit of time and start to think of positive things that I have done and am thankful for. I will often do this by going on a short walk.

I have an individual who I had coached who had had a really rough go of things. In fact, the first day we met, he told me that he and his wife were getting a divorce. Whoa, what a way to start a coaching relationship! A couple of months later he was hoping that they could reconcile. He was so hopeful, but then he sent me a text after he met with her one morning and he told me that the divorce was for sure going to happen. He asked me how he should not let his personal life interfere with his professional life. My response was, "The answer to your question is very simple. It is a choice. You move forward, not backwards. You give yourself permission to be down and out and angry and sorry for yourself for no longer than a week. That week starts today!! Next Friday, as we prepare for Christmas, you move forward in both your personal and professional life. You choose what both of those look like. Then on Christmas you take time by yourself and write down all the things you are blessed by. You give thanks for those blessings and then you use your blessings to propel you forward."

You see, we choose whether we are successful or not. He had that choice, and he wasn't sure he had the ability to make that choice. In fact, we all have that ability, and so no matter what you may be going through you can choose to be successful. You can choose to thrive.

Michael Hyatt, Founder and CEO of Michael Hyatt & Co., says, "success requires help and usually lots of it."[6] "Instead of random relationships, we can create communities that help everyone involved achieve their goals together."[7] I really love this thought by Hyatt. I used to think that I had to do everything on my own to be successful. I now realize that this is impossible and very arrogant. To think we can do everything on our own without anyone's help is ludicrous. Working with other people to help one another achieve their goals is the best way to get things done. We all have different strengths and by working together we can utilize each of them to do great things. By doing this we can totally thrive.

Success is not only a journey, it is something we must work on every day. Yes, we must also work with others and try to improve the lives of others. Getting better each day and serving others each day brings us joy, happiness, and peace. There is no better feeling than being done with a long day knowing that you moved closer to your objective and in doing so you helped and served a whole lot of people. It doesn't matter if the people you served were your spouse, children, customers, friends, co-workers, or individuals at a

---

[6]   Michael Hyatt, *Your Best Year Ever*, (Grand Rapids, MI: Baker Books, 2018) p. 179

[7]   *Ibid.*, p. 181

soup kitchen. What matters is that at the end of the day you can say you helped someone else.

Zig Ziglar is one of the most well-known self-help and personal productivity people ever to walk the face of this earth. He was such a positive person that it was absolutely contagious. I have been blessed to read his books and listen to his audio recordings. I was also very blessed to see him speak in person, and that was at a point very late in his life when he was doing engagements with his daughter. Even the great Zig relied on others to help him reach success. He said, "Your success and your happiness start with you... You already have the ability necessary for success."[8] For him it was all about attitude. Everyone has their own unique abilities to lead them to success. However, if you are not willing to get up every day and do it, then you will never, ever be a success.

I believe that Brian Tracy, a Canadian-American motivational public speaker and self-help author, sums up success very well: "Successful people have success habits and unsuccessful people do not. Success is the ability to live your life the way you want to, doing what you most enjoy, surrounded by people who you admire and respect."[9] There are countless people in our world who are the latter. They have absolutely no success habits. In fact this is probably the biggest thing that separates them from those who are successful. If they would just form some success habits, they would be on their path to a successful and meaningful life.

---

[8] Zig Ziglar, *See You At The Top*, (Gretna, Louisiana: Pelican Publishing Co, 1982) p 40

[9] "The Power of Habit: 7 Steps to Successful Habits - Brian Tracy." https://www.briantracy.com/success/personal/op/the-power-of-habit.html. 2.

I am so blessed in my life. I have success habits that I live each day. Sure, there are days when I fail, but I would estimate it is less than 5% of the days in a particular year. I am very intentional with living my success habits. I am also very blessed to be able to live my life the way I want it to be lived. I enjoy my career in that I get to truly help people achieve their financial objectives. I was put on this earth to help people and I get to do that. I am also blessed to spend time almost each day with my beloved wife and my children. As my children get older and they have begun leaving our home it does become more challenging, but not impossible. It just requires intentionality, and I am that way with my children. I also am blessed with a great group of friends that I spend a lot of time with. I am successful and I am still on this journey. I was made to thrive and I will do what I can each day to accomplish that.

My goal is to help you in being a success. I want you to thrive as well. I want you to be able to form the success habits that you need to serve others and do the things you want to do. It really is a very simple process, but its up to you to take action. I am going to give you the steps necessary to help you thrive. It starts with your mission in life. If you don't have a mission, you cannot start down your road to success.

Pillar One & Practice One: Mission Statement

have a very simple mission statement for my life and it consists of just one sentence. Here it is: To improve the lives of others by serving them with great passion. That is it. It sets out for me the why of what I do in everything. I have a deep desire to do everything I can while I am alive on this earth to help people. Helping and serving others is something that really drives me! Everything that I do in my life is driven from my personal mission statement. If my wife, Cyndi, and I have to decide about doing something and it does not fall under my personal mission statement then I am not going to do it. Now, the truth is that sometimes I have done some things after being asked to do them and have said "Yes" in spite of the fact that whatever is being asked of me does not really fall under my mission statement. This is almost always due to my huge ego and how flattered I am to be asked.

I really believe that everyone needs to have their own mission statement. Many companies have mission statements, so why not individuals? I also think it is a good idea for families to have family mission statements. A mission statement should show why you do the things you do in your life. A mission is what motivates you each day to do what you do. Without a mission we are just swimming upstream, trying to figure out why we are even in the river in the first place.

Author and speaker Simon Sinek says, "People don't buy what you do, they buy why you do it."[10] So, why are you in business? Ultimately, the only way you can succeed at what you are doing is to actually accomplish your why. I love how Sinek ties back our mission to success. Again, success is a journey, and for Sinek it is the continual journey of accomplishing your mission over and over again: day after day, hour after hour, minute after minute.

Take a note of my personal mission statement again, "To improve the lives of others by serving them with great passion." By just reading this it is obvious that I will never be able to accomplish my mission because no matter what age I am in my life or what part of my career I am in, I can always continue to improve the lives of others by serving them with great passion. A personal mission statement ought to be a general, overarching standard to measure success that can permeate into every area of your life, no matter what age or what season of life you happen to be in.

I would like to think that I accomplish my mission every day that I work with my clients. I truly believe that when I meet them in my office, speak to them on the phone or have an email exchange with them that I am actually improving their lives by my help. You better believe that I am also help-

---

[10]   Simon Sinek, *Start With Why* (New York: Penguin Group, 2009), p. 41

ing them with great passion. The key for me personally is that I am trying to put their needs first.

Dave Ramsey—author, radio host, and businessman—says, "A mission statement is who we are as a people, and you really need to know that. Our mission statement helps us to stay on track and concentrate on what we are good at. Developing your mission statement forces you to decide in advance who you are. Great companies figure out their strengths and calling and stick to them. Focusing on the main thing, and keeping the main thing the main thing, causes individuals to be more likely to win."[11]

I read my personal mission statement at least once a week. I also share it with others at least once a week. The reason I do this is because of what Ramsey talks about in that our mission statement will help us stay on track. If you wake up in the morning and are wondering why you woke up in the morning and maybe feel like steering off the tracks, look no further than your mission statement. Keeping it in front of myself is a great reminder. Also, by sharing it with friends and family they can help to keep me accountable to what I say is important to me.

I also think that I am accomplishing my mission when I serve Cyndi and my kids. I love to spend time with all of them, and every day I try to help them be the best they can be by also serving them with great passion.

Whenever I serve on boards or volunteer for other activities I am also trying to accomplish my mission. Another aspect of my life that my Mission Statement filters into is

---

[11] Dave Ramsey, *Entreleadership*, (New York, NY: Harper Books, 2011) pp 28-29

my friendships. I invest very heavily in my friendships so that I can help improve their lives by serving them with great passion. One of my hopes is that in every area of my life and in everything that I do, I am trying to achieve and live out my mission. Even my own self-care of my spiritual and physical growth helps me to accomplish my mission. If I don't take care of myself physically, emotionally, spiritually, and mentally, then I will be an utter failure in trying to accomplish my mission.

John Maxwell says that one aspect of success is to know that "each of us has a purpose for which we were created."[12] Why were you created? What is your mission? What provides you with the most joy? What drives you to stay awake instead of pressing that snooze button when you wake up in the morning? Maxwell, in his book, quotes Albert Schweitzer who quipped, "The purpose of human life is to serve and to show compassion and the will to help others."[13] If you look at anyone who has been successful and seems to enjoy the journey of success, they have all had this similar mindset: the mindset to serve and help others.

Everyone's Mission Statement is going to be a little bit different. But each Mission Statement, if it is a success-driven one, ought to be accompanied with the ideals of helping others and filling that hole in the heart with the lifting up and serving of others. Not only will others be helped, but you just might find yourself being filled. The chasm of selfishness will vanish as it is filled with a mission of self-

---

[12] Maxwell, *3 Things Successful People Do*, p. 13.
[13] *Ibid*, p 17

lessness. A Mission Statement ought to encourage that sort of lifestyle.

When I read the above two quotes in Maxwell's book it made me think long and hard about what provides me with the most joy as well as service to others. I am not saying that your personal mission statement has to be mine. Ultimately, it needs to define you and what is important to you. It has to be something that drives you and gives you great joy!

Life can be very difficult. There are moments where everything just seems to be falling apart on us. It seems we simply cannot make a good decision. We seem to be failing at work, our marriage, and our family. These are typically just for a season, but while we are going through it, it seems like everything is just crashing down upon us. It is helpful to be reminded by John Maxwell as he says, "More than anything else, what keeps a person going in the midst of adversity is having a sense of purpose. It is the fuel that powers persistence."[14]

This is so true! I have had many moments in my life where I feel everything is just spiraling out of control. When that happens, I go back to focusing on my mission and what is most important to me. Just going back and reflecting on that helps me to get through whatever seems to be bringing me down. I then realize that it is only for a time, and as long as I continue to persevere then all will be well. I will continue to serve others with great passion and by doing this I will truly have joy in my life.

---

[14] John Maxwell, *Failing Forward*, (Nashville: Thomas Nelson, Inc, 2000), p. 170

I have also had many a friend who has had a rough go in a seemingly strenuous season of their life. For them it has seemed like the entire world is stacked up against them as they looked up at the tidal wave of overwhelm. Often, they did not think they would be able to get through and survive it. Tragically, it was very difficult for them to even see what their sense of purpose was during that arduous time. However, if they remember in these moments their mission in life, then hopefully that Mission can be a guidepost to set them in the right direction so that they can once again find that purpose that they long for and sometimes have lost.

Maxwell has more encouraging words when he says, "Believe in your mission... Our life's mission cannot be borrowed from someone else."[15] What does this mean? Well, first of all, you actually have to believe in what you think your purpose is. It's one thing to think it. It's entirely another matter to actually internalize and believe it. If you don't believe in what you think, then what's the point? You would probably be better off not having a Mission Statement at all. Secondly, you cannot just copy, paste, and use someone else's mission statement. It has to be *your* statement, otherwise it just won't work. Its pretty much like plagiarizing, not in the fact that its illegal, but in the fact that if you just copy and use someone else's idea, it doesn't really mean anything to your heart and isn't produced organically by you. If you are trying to accomplish someone else's mission then that may be a great thing, but it won't bring you true joy and happiness. It will likely just help that other person accom-

---

[15] John Maxwell, *Intentional Living, Choosing A Life That Matters* (New York: Hachette Book Group, 2017), p. 68.

plish their mission. Your mission is something that you have to have great passion about. Your Mission Statement must be *yours!*

Maxwell also has more words on Mission when he says, "If you want to make a difference and live a life of significance, you must tap into your why."[16] What's the use of doing the "what" if we do not even know our "why"? We need to find our purpose in life, and this is our "why." Maxwell goes on to say, "When you start your day with your why, you will find yourself continually doing things that inspire you... Knowing your why allows you to focus more on others and less on yourself."[17] There's that idea of filling that inward chasm of selfishness through acts of service and selflessness again.

I can say that without a shadow of doubt that Maxwell is dead on with this last point. On the days I start off with my "why," there is no doubt that those are the days that I am most intentional with my day. The days when I am in touch with and have tapped into my "why" are also the days that I am better able to serve others, clients, family, friends—you name it! When I start my day and become consumed with myself, then these are the days that I am most miserable. Sure, I need to take care of myself, but ultimately, if I have a day that is not about serving others then I will have a very bad day. Again, your mission may be different, but I promise you that if you are very intentional with your day and moving through your mission, then you will have a great day; I guarantee it!

---

[16] *Ibid.*, p. 79.
[17] *Ibid.*, pp. 80-81.

So how does one go about writing their own personal mission statement? I really struggled with this question for years, but after reading some of the authors that I have quoted in this chapter, it just came to me. It has to be something that is very important to you. It is something that drives you each day. It is your "why," your reason for living.

I think the first step is to take an hour or a few hours of retreat by yourself and really put some thought into what you enjoy, or what provides you with joy, energy, and is life-giving for you. If you had to put one thing down that motivates you to get up out of your bed each morning and to really get going then what would that be? I have shared my "why," my mission, with you. You have to figure out what it is for you.

You may be a person who is very involved in the medical community. Maybe you are a nurse and care deeply about making people feel better. Not only do you do this in your career, but you also notice yourself always trying to make your spouse, children, and friends feel better. If someone is feeling down or sick you are the first person to offer to help them get better. Your mission may be to every day help people feel better. It can be as simple as that. If helping others to feel better is what drives you and is something that you are passionate about, then great! It's your Mission Statement.

A Mission Statement does not have to be some elaborate paragraph about how you are going to serve mankind. Sure, it can be. In fact for several years mine was a paragraph. The theme was the same in helping to improve the lives of others, but I was very specific in my paragraph on who that would be. It was my wife, children, clients, support team members, extended family, church family, friends, and greater community. Ultimately, I decided to just simplify it. Every morning, I didn't have the time or where-with-all to just think of that long, drawn out paragraph if I was questioning my "why." The change to an easy, quick to remember statement helped me to hone in on my "why": my mission.

You may have a career as a Garbage Collector. You may love knowing that you are able to make your community or the world a cleaner place. You may be the type of person that is always picking up after everyone else. You may be the first to volunteer when anyone needs a helping hand in cleaning out their garage, picking up limbs and sticks in their yard. Cleaning may be something that totally drives you. Your mission could read, "Doing everything I can to make the world a cleaner place by helping to pick up the messes in people's lives." That would be an amazing Mission Statement. Its broad enough to be a part of every area of life. It's not long and drawn out, and it is focused.

I could go on and on with a variety of examples, but I think you may be getting the point. Again, you cannot borrow someone else's mission statement. It has to be *your* "why." It has to be something that you are passionate about.

I do know one very important thing about Mission Statements. If it is your statement and you are very intentional about it each day, then you will have joy, peace, and happiness. You will be successful. The journey upon which you find and experience success will be quite enjoyable and you will have less and less stress and anxiety. Why? Because you have a standard, a weighing mechanism, a scale upon which you can guide your life when making commitments, decisions, and deciding what is most important to you. You will have a great life and you will feel a great sense of purpose, not to mention the fact that you feel good about yourself along the way, which is always a plus! Sure, you will have days that don't go so well, but most days, hours, and minutes will be quite rewarding. You will have a purpose, you will have a tremendous impact on others, and you will be successful.

So, what are you waiting for? Stop reading this book for a few hours and get to work on it. Tap into your "why" and form your own personal Mission Statement. Take that time by yourself and reflect. Finally, once you have put something together, share it with the people closest to you. Ask for their input and modify as necessary. You can do this! You were made to thrive!!!

Mission is the first pillar to success. The second is just as important, as you will begin to define your future. In order to continue on your journey you need to have an idea on what the destination will be. Your journey and level of success will take you closer to that destination. The second pillar of success is Vision.

Pillar Two & Practice Two: Vision

W here would we be without a Vision? Let's delve into the Good Book to see what it has to say. "Where there is no vision, the people perish," says Proverbs 29:18. Now that is a strong statement. Let's take a look at that again. "Where there is *no vision*, the people *perish*". The statement doesn't read that the people will fail or that they will stumble a little bit. The statement clearly states that they will *perish*. Perish! That is a pretty dire result of having no vision, don't you think? So…it would probably be a great idea for us to put together a vision so we can avoid the alternative. Who wants to perish today? Not me!

Let's take a look at the differences between Mission and Vision, because the two can be confused with each other sometimes. Whereas Mission is your **why**, Vision is your **what** or **where**. It is **where** you are headed in the future, **what** you want your future to look like. It is where you want to be. What does that look like for you? If you happen to be a part of a team or a company, then the team or company's vision is what gives you and all of your team members something to focus on in the long term. It gives everyone something to shoot or strive for, a certain destination to get to. A vision has to be something that everyone on the team gets excited about so they can all row in the same direction with the goal of achieving that vision. P.J. Fleck, current Head Football Coach of the University of Minnesota, is famous for telling his players to row the boat. When good old P.J. parades the phrase, "Row the boat!", what he means by that is he wants everyone rowing in the same direction toward their vision.

I love how Napoleon Hill, a renowned personal productivity author, talks about Vision. He says, "Whatever you want to achieve must be a consuming passion of your life in a burning desire you must be willing to stake your entire future on your desire to win."[18] I mean, this vision thing is something that you really, really want to accomplish. It's a place you are always wanting to get to. You are willing to stake everything on it to get it done. Hill goes on to say, "Fix in your mind the exact goal that you have. Determine exactly what you intend to give in return for what you desire. Establish a definite date on when you will possess what you desire. Create a defining plan for carrying out your desire. Begin this at once. Write out a clear and concise statement of what you intend to do."[19]

Napoleon Hill believes that it is important to be very clear as well as concise in what it is that you want to accomplish. It cannot be something that is vague but must be very clear. I also like that he suggests that it be kept concise. It should not be something that is long and drawn out and

---

[18] Napoleon Hill, *Think and Grow Rich*, Ch. 2 (Meriden, CT: The Ralston Society, 1937), p. 21.

[19] *Ibid., pp. 22-23.*

goes on and on and on. It needs to be something that comes easily to your mind when you think of your vision because it isn't something that is overly complicated. The vision also has to be time-bound. There must be a specific date and time by which you want to have x, y, and z accomplished or arrived at. A vision can't be something that does not have an end date because if it doesn't, then you won't take the necessary actions to get it done.

In the summer of 2018, I was blessed to go on a Mission Trip to San Pedro, Belize. I went with my four oldest children along with two other families and a priest we are all friends with. It was an amazing experience and I will never forget it. One of the things that we were asked to assist with while we were on the island was helping the church we were working with to do some strategic planning. We spent a lot of time on having each pillar of the church come up with a vision for their group. Cyndi and I were able to go back to the island a few months after our mission trip and the fruit that we saw come out of our mission trip was inspiring. By the time my wife and I went back to the island, we saw clearly that the church was fulfilling the vision that we had helped them set up just a few short months prior. I believe that helping each group of the church to come up with a vision was key to the success of the church family.

Our friend John Maxwell compares a vision to a dream. Maxwell says, "A dream gives us direction,...it acts like a compass...A dream helps us to prioritize."[20] The actions that we take each day should be based upon what our dream or vision is. Think about a dream you may have. What you

---

[20]   Maxwell, *3 Things Successful People Do*, pp. 25-26.

want for your life. What you envision your future to look like. That's your vision! If you can envision it and it goes along with your mission, then what are you waiting for? Write down that Vision! Without this dream or vision we are just meandering about with no direction in our life. The vision is our "Due North" and once we have that arrow pointing us along the road of success, we can then assemble our days, weeks, and even months to go in that direction.

Brian Moran and Michael Lennington write at great length about vision. They are the creators of the 12 Week Year which is a system of organizing your year into 12 weeks at a time for your goals. Their book, *The 12 Week Year*, was very instrumental in helping me to come up with my vision. They provide detailed information on how to put together your vision. "The first step is to create a personal vision, a vision that clearly captures and articulates what you want in life...when the task seems too difficult or unpleasant, you can reconnect with your personal objectives and vision."[21] It really is quite simple. You just can't be successful in your career, family, friendships and community if you do not have a vision that is compelling. Compelling thoughts, dreams and ideas stir in us the desire to act. Moran and Lennington agree with Maxwell and Hill that you need to have short term objectives that will lead you to your vision. It is all a part of the process or journey—the journey of success.

Moran and Lennington go on to say, "The vision must be compelling and something you are emotionally con-nected with. Your personal vision should cover all areas of

---

[21] Brian P Moran & Michael Lennington, *The 12 Week Year*, (Hoboken, NJ: John Wiley & Sons, Inc, 2013), pp. 21-22.

your life, including spiritual, relationships, family, income, lifestyle, health, and community."[22] This is critically important. Because they state that the vision should cover all of these areas, it may become difficult to follow Hill's suggestion of keeping your vision concise. My suggestion is that you don't necessarily need one vision to cover every area, but modify what Moran and Lennington have laid out and have a separate vision for each of these areas.

Moran and Lennington do encourage this broader vision, which they call an Aspirational Vision. However, the way they encourage you to write it out does separate all of the areas. The important thing is that for all of the areas of your life, it is time bound for some time in the future and that future is the exact same time for each area. It keeps things consistent. They further say, "The most powerful visions address and align your personal aspirations with your professional dreams. Your life vision gives traction and relevance to your business. Your vision should be big enough that it makes you feel a little bit uncomfortable."[23]

Yep, a vision needs to be challenging. If it is not, then it won't be compelling—and remember, we want our visions to be compelling and exciting. Challenges excite people and challenges that people want to overcome are exciting. The person striving to thrive will work and take the necessary action steps to achieve the vision. This is because the vision is exciting, challenging, and compelling. Your vision needs to be something that is really going to push you to your limits. If it was easy then it would not take sacrifice,

[22] *Ibid.*, p 21.
[23] *Ibid., p 79.*

diligence, hard work, and even pain. It would also then be something that you wouldn't be excited about accomplishing. You would then just be stuck in the ho-hum of daily living without any direction. You would end up perishing, and who wants that to happen?

Here is my Aspirational Vision for when I am 60:

1. Physically- I am in good health, with a weight of 165 pounds and working out at least five days a week.

2. Spiritually- I am fully serving God and furthering His Kingdom by being involved in ministries that do this. I am fully following His will for my life. I start each day with Morning Prayer, Bible Reading, and Journaling. I also pray a Rosary and Chaplet of Divine Mercy daily, and spending time with Him daily at Mass. I also make a weekly Holy Hour and go to Confession at least every other week. I am a light to others I come into contact with so that they may come to know His love for them.

3. Personal- I am happy and full of joy and peace. I am reading two books per month to help me improve as a husband, father, leader, Advisor or other vocational reading. I am also listening to a variety of podcasts. Cyndi and I, along with our kids, are able to do the things we enjoy most doing as a family. Cyndi and I are able to travel together with our kids. We are able to go out regularly to restaurants and recreational activities such as movies, baseball games, theatre, hiking, and our kids' or grandkids' activities.

4. Relationships- Cyndi and I have a weekly date, and we travel together at least once per quarter. We have a loving marriage and strive to serve one another daily above ourselves. We talk daily and share with each other the blessings we have had as well as those things that are bothering each of us. We enjoy spending time with our kids and they enjoy spending time with us. I spend time with each child twice per month, even if only by phone, and daily with my youngest son Joseph. We come together as a family for a family meal at least once each week. Our children continue to grow in their frailty and strengths and further God's Kingdom. I spend time with my parents if they are still living twice per month. I have close, dynamic, and fun relationships with the people who are important in my family's life. These are our extended family and close friends. We spend time together and we assist our family and friends when they need us.

5. Financially- We have a very nice lifestyle. We are not worried about our finances and because of that we can enjoy the blessings God has provided to us. We are entirely debt free and because of this we are able to give more to charity and to our friends and family. In everything that we have been blessed with we are more than happy to have others enjoy this blessing as well. Because my income is more than enough to satisfy our needs and wants it allows me to take more time off to serve in other

ways. I am financially independent, meaning I don't have to work.

6. Professionally- Working no more than 3 ½ days per week. I have 300 Financial Services Clients and 20 Coaching Clients. I meet with six Financial Service Clients each week, and five coaching clients. I lead my team and organization. I am helping them to grow in their careers and life. We have team meetings on Monday mornings.

Moran and Lennington also discuss what to do after you have established the Aspirational Vision. Once you have crafted your vision you need to do three action steps. "Share it with others... Stay in touch with your vision... Live with intention."[24] I have already expressed the importance of sharing your mission with others. Sharing filters into this vision part of your life too. I would encourage you to take the time each day to reflect on the progress you are making each day. Intentional living is also key! If you don't design each day with your vision in mind then you will never reach it. I will touch more on intentionality later, but for now, just let me emphasize that your whole day should be intentional.

This really is what it's all about. Moran and Lennington give practical actions that we all must take to move our vision from just a dream to a reality. Sharing it with others is just a great way to hold yourself accountable to what you said was important to you. If your closest friends and family or coworkers know what your vision is then they can be a great source of reminder to you every once in a

---

[24] *Ibid.*, pp. 87-88.

while, whether you ask them or if you yourself lose sight of what your Vision is. I have shared mine with those closest to me and now I have shared it with you. You all can hold me accountable to practice what I preach!

Speaking of accountability, reviewing your vision daily can be very helpful. It can be so easy to just put it away on the top shelf of your home office, let it collect dust, and never look at it again. If you do this though then you will be sure to **perish**. Out of sight, out of mind. Your dreams won't materialize, and you will be stuck in fantasy land forever! The solution to the "write it down and never look at it" syndrome is to review, review, review! If you are not constantly reminding yourself of what your vision is then you will have no chance of achieving it. Once you review this daily for many, many weeks then you may end up having it memorized. Even if that is true it is still important to reflect on it each week moving forward. Maybe even include it into your weekly review and reflect on what you did the day before to try to get closer to the vision.

The last point they make is being very intentional about examining the progress you have made each day. I would also be very intentional with writing down things you will do the next day to help you get closer to your vision. If you do not constantly create and follow your road map then it just won't work out. You have to write things down for each day so you can have it in front of your face. By looking at it, putting action steps down for each day, and then acting upon them there is no doubt in my mind that you will be successful.

This whole exercise in visioning doesn't just have to be for you as an individual. Starting with yourself to make sure your own house is in order is a great start, but you can also do this with your team, company, and family. Within your professional life, if you are in a division of a company or just work closely with one or two people, you can create a vision with that team of what your dreams for that specific team you are a part of. Create a vision for the team, something that everyone can get behind and strive for. Take a page out of P.J. Fleck's book: grab an oar and row the boat. Review the Vision daily or weekly with your team and reflect on the progress you are making.

The vision for a company doesn't have to always be about revenue or profit. It could be, but it could also be something else, such as: by 2025 we want to have 500 clients. That is a risky and aggressive vision if you only have 250 clients and have only five years to get there. If you are a Financial Advisor who specializes in Retirement Planning, the vision may be we want to have had 500 new Retirement Plans prepared for our Baby Boomer clients in ten years. From there you then need to create the action steps to make sure you get to those 500 plans.

You may be the director of a day care center. Your vision may be that you want to help 30 children learn to read by 2023. Then you work with your team to figure out what needs to take place to help you achieve that objective. I really believe that it is important to share practical ideas for how to put together your vision statement. In order to do that I will turn directly to Rory Vaden, a speaker and author. He says, "What do you see for your future? What matters most to you? What would you want your perfect life to look like? What is it that you want to have? What things do you want to do?"[25] These are great questions to reflect upon as you put together your vision statement. I did and it helped me tremendously.

Take the time now to get started. Hopefully, you have already put together your mission statement. Now it's time to take things to the next level. You were made to thrive. Show others on paper what that is going to look like for you.

The next section of this book will assist you in moving your vision closer to reality with the practical steps and ideas you need to get there. I will walk you through the third Pillar of Success: Goals!

---

[25] Rory Vaden, *Take The Stairs*, (New York: Penguin Group, Inc, 2012), p. 97.

Pillar Three & Practice Three: Goals

n the previous chapter I spoke at length about the importance of having a vision. Remember, a vision is the long term objective you have for your life, and the objective or objectives can cover several areas of your life. Well, a vision without some clearly defined goals is meaningless. In order to make your vision become a reality, you need to have concrete goals that you can achieve in order to keep the personal needle moving. Without goals your vision and your dreams will never happen. It's not just like you can dream it and that dream then exists in reality. No, there must be action and work that goes into making that vision a reality. The work can be seen in the goals you formulate for yourself. There have been a whole lot of people who have had a whole lot to say on the subject of goals, so throughout this entire chapter I will be taking a deep dive on what others have said about goal setting.

Setting goals gets you started on your journey of success. Zig Ziglar says, "With definite goals you release your own power, and things start happening...There are seven different kinds of goals: physical, mental, spiritual, personal, family, career, and financial."[26] Think about this for a second. If you never had something to shoot for then you would likely just sit around all day and do nothing. That is why goals give you this power and because of the goals, things do begin happening because you are going after something and taking the actions to get there.

John Maxwell talks about how setting goals and planning for how to achieve them is the first step to get to success. In order to achieve your goals it is important to break them down into more manageable objectives or steps. He says, "Goals draw out your sense of purpose."[27] "Your goals map your actions. Your actions create results. The results bring you success."[28] Maxwell also affirms as many experts on goal setting that goals must be written, personal, specific, achievable, measurable, and time sensitive.[29] You cannot be successful in life without having goals. They help to get you to your dreams because they draw out your sense of purpose as Maxwell said.

Let's all jump into Tony's Time Machine and go back once again to when I was a high school athlete. I want to use my running goals as an example of what Maxwell is talking about. I wanted to be the State Champion at the State Championship Cross Country Meet. It was definitely personal since the first word of the goal was "I." It was very specific: I wanted to be the State Champion. It was also measurable: I was either going to be the State Champion or

---

[26] Zig Ziglar, *See You At The Top*, (Gretna, Louisiana: Pelican Publishing Co, 1982), p. 157.

[27] John Maxwell, *3 Things Successful People Do*, p. 67.

[28] *Ibid.*, p 70.

[29] *Ibid,* pp 74-75

just be like everyone else. It was also time sensitive, because my goal was specific to a certain date, the date of the State Meet. Now, the only thing it may not have been was achievable. But, on second thought, it actually was achievable. As I said earlier in this book I beat the State Champion the very next year in my first College Cross Country Meet. The problem with my goal in High School is that I am not sure that I actually believed I could do it. If I would have, then I may have actually written it down and shared it with others.

Dave Ramsey sums it up well, "Goals force practical steps in your life to make your dreams come true. Goals have to be specific, measurable, have a time limit, and be your goals, not someone else's. Goals must also be in writing, which is where most people skip."[30] Ramsey is also a huge fan of Zig Ziglar and agrees that your goals should cover all the spokes of Zig's Wheel of Life. The spokes of goal setting are career, financial, spiritual, physical, intellectual, family, and social. This sounds pretty similar to the life domains I used in the previous chapter on your Vision.

Ramsey is very clear on the path to achieving your dreams. Most people would call what he has laid out SMART Goals which are goals that are specific, measurable, actionable, realistic, and time bound. Stating that you want to lose weight is not a SMART goal. However, stating that you want to lose 10 pounds by the end of the year likely would be. It is clearly specific, something that can be measured, takes action, and is definitely time bound. Now, if you weigh 50 pounds then it may not be wise to lose 10 pounds and it also may not be realistic, but if you weigh 200 pounds then

---

[30] Dave Ramsey, *Entreleadership*, (New York, NY: Harper Books, 2011) p 31

it probably is realistic. One more important thing here is what Ramsey says about a goal being your own. You cannot come up with a dream or vision and then have someone else give you the goals to get there. They have to be **your** goals.

Authors Brian Moran and Michael Lennington, also affirm what Ramsey has said, "Tactics are the daily to-do's that drive attainment of your goals. They must be specific, actionable, and include dates and assigned responsibilities."[31] This last part is critical. You can have everything else in place for your goal, but if you don't have tactics or assigned responsibilities then there is no way you will achieve your goals, your vision or your dreams. You can't just sit there. You need to get moving and work hard for it.

Process

It is important to have a process in place for your goals. The first part of the process starts with actually writing your goals down. This is where most people fail in that they never write them down so they are never in front of them to remind them what they actually are. Think about this. When it comes to business, a business plan is not just something that is verbalized. A business plan is always written down. Why would you not do the same with your goals? It just makes sense!

---

[31] Brian P. Moran & Michael Lennington, *The 12 Week Year* (Hoboken, NJ: John Wiley & Sons, Inc, 2013), p. 28.

Brian Buffini, Founder of Buffini and Company, says, "You should write short term goals to get you started."[32] Buffini also talks about how a "written goal clarifies what you really want, creates objectives on which to focus your energy, and it becomes a lighthouse in the storm."[33] What a great analogy that is. If a lighthouse is not present in a storm then the ships and boats would not be able to see the coast and the rocks all around it. They would then crash into the rocks and tragedy would strike. We all need lighthouses to help us avoid our pitfalls and tragedy.

Michael Hyatt, former CEO of Thomas Nelson Publishers, is one of the foremost experts on goal setting today. Hyatt shares the importance of writing down your goals: "Committing your goals to writing is foundational for at least five reasons: first, it forces you to clarify what you want. Second, writing down goals helps you overcome resistance. Third, it motivates you to take action. Fourth, it filters other opportunities. Fifth, it enables you to see and celebrate your progress."[34] Did you see that, maybe re-read what Hyatt says. The first thing he says is that it is foundational to write. That means you absolutely need it. If you don't put in a foundation when building a house then it will ultimately collapse, so without writing your goals down then all will also collapse. I also really love his fourth reason, the idea that it will filter other opportunities. If you don't have your goals written down then you will likely say yes

---

[32] Brian Buffini, *Emigrant Edge* (New York, NY: Howard Books, 2017), p, 199,

[33] *Ibid.,* pp. 200-201.

[34] Michael Hyatt, *Your Best Year Ever* (Grand Rapids, MI: Baker Books, 2018), pp. 105,107.

to opportunities presented to you that actually could derail you from achieving your goals. You may help someone else achieve their goals, but it may detract you from your own.

For much of my professional life I had been very guilty of violating Hyatt's fourth reason for committing your goals to writing. I never wrote down my goals, and as a result I actually never did filter through opportunities. Anytime an opportunity would come up for me I would just seize it without even thinking through whether this would help get me closer to what my vision was. Heck, the real problem was that I didn't even have a vision. I can't emphasize enough how important it is to write down your goals based on your vision. Until recently I never did it for my professional life or my personal life. That had been a huge mistake. It may be the number one reason it really took me so long to get to where I am today.

Zig Ziglar also touches on the importance of writing down your goals. Ziglar says, "You should commit to paper the things you want to be, do, and have....Write them down and list them in the order of their importance."[35] He further says, "Once you've arranged your goals in the order of their importance, you should list the obstacles that stand between you and your objectives,...formulate a plan to overcome them and set a time schedule."[36] Zig goes even further here. He thinks that we should not only write down our goals, but we should also be thinking about all of those things that can get in the way of our goals. This is so important that

---

[35] Zig Ziglar, *See You At The Top*, (Gretna, Louisiana: Pelican Publishing Co, 1982), p. 171.

[36] *Ibid,*, p, 171,

he even tells us that we have to have a plan in place just to overcome the obstacles. That way, when difficulties in life seem to be flying at you, you will know what to do to deal with them properly. Don't forget to schedule a time to work through those obstacles so you are better prepared for them when they come up. This will allow you to continue on your journey of success.

I have already touched on what a SMART Goal is. I mentioned Michael Hyatt earlier and he actually dives much deeper for how to put together a goal. He calls a good goal a SMARTER Goal. For a goal to be successful he says it needs seven attributes rather than the five of a SMART Goal. From his book Your Best Year Ever, he states they must be:

1. Specific, the goal must be specific. The more specific the goal, the more likely we are to engage our focus, creativity, intellect, and persistence.
2. Measurable, the goal has built-in criteria you can measure yourself against.
3. Actionable, or what you are going to do; you have to be able to do something.
4. Risky, usually the R stands for realistic. By doing this you set the bar too low. Take a little risk by setting it higher and something that will challenge and stretch us.
5. Time-keyed, connected to a deadline, frequency, or a time trigger. Set seven to ten goals per year but only two to three per quarter.

6. Exciting, it inspires you. Only an exciting goal can access the internal motivation you need to stay the course and achieve your goal.

7. Relevant to you and your life.[37]

In essence, he both adds to and modifies the SMART Goals. He modifies it by taking the R which normally means realistic and changes it to risky. I really like this. Sometimes realistic is too easy. In my previous example, a 200-pound man to losing 10 pounds may be pretty realistic, but it probably won't really push him.

I have to tell you that I hate the idea of making a goal that is a bit risky. When I set out to do something I want to actually do it. I would prefer to set a goal I know I can reach. However, making a risky goal stretches me even further and actually helps me to get to my ultimate vision even faster.

Hyatt then adds the two at the end. Exciting is the E in SMARTER. Of course, why would we not want to set a goal that is exciting and inspires us? Also, if they are our own goals rather than someone else's then they should inspire us. Finally, relevance is important. I can't have a goal to join the PGA Tour—this would be totally irrelevant to me. Now, if my goal was to get to a 28 handicap then maybe it would be relevant. On second thought, maybe even that one is a stretch!

If I was to use a current running goal that hits on the E and the R of Hyatt's SMARTER goals I may say I want to run a 5K in 19:00 by June 1st. I am getting close to 50

[37] Michael Hyatt, *Your Best Year Ever*, (Grand Rapids, MI: Baker Books, 2018), pp. 107-117.

years of age so 19:00 is a bit risky for me. About two years ago I ran a 5K in 19:40. To take 40 more seconds off in just the next six months would definitely be risky, but it is also relevant to me, a soon-to-be 50 male runner. It would no longer be relevant for me to try and run a 5k in 15:30. It just probably isn't even possible at my age and state in life.

Ziglar also gives us some good characteristics of goals that have some similarities. "We need some big goals. Some of our goals must be big, because it takes a big goal to create the excitement necessary for maximum excitement."[38] The second characteristic is it must be long-range.[39] The third characteristic is that goals must be daily; if you don't have daily objectives, you qualify as a dreamer. The fourth characteristic is that goals must be specific."[40]

Some interesting takes from Ziglar here. He agrees with Hyatt with a goal that is exciting to you. However, he goes further in stating that it must be a really big goal. Heck yeah, the bigger the goal, the more exciting it will be. Ziglar also tells us that this goal must be a long range goal; I am thinking about vision here. Then he says that we must have goals that are daily, and these are the types of things that will help us to achieve our vision.

Brian Buffini also tells us that midterm goals will keep us going. The point is we cannot just have some long term vision and not have much shorter term goals. These goals

---

[38] Zig Ziglar, *See You At The Top*, (Gretna, Louisiana: Pelican Publishing Co, 1982), p. 161.
[39] *Ibid.,* p. 164
[40] *Ibid.*, p. 165

will drive us closer to our vision. He finally says, "Long term goals give you hope."[41]

Remember a little earlier in this chapter I discussed what Ziglar said about writing down goals. He was also very insistent about writing down a plan to deal with those obstacles that come up because without a plan we will not be able to overcome the obstacles. Ziglar is not the only one to comment on this. John Maxwell says, "Come up with a plan to achieve your goals. Develop new strategies to succeed."[42] Again, it is the strategies that are written down that will help you. Once your goals are established Moran and Lennington emphasize, "You need to write tactics...The tactics start with a verb and are complete sentences."[43]

Types of Goals

I have already shared about the different spokes in Ziglar's Wheel of Life. He and others such as Moran and Lennington have dissected the importance of having goals that cover various areas of your life. In concurrence with them, I strongly believe that this is vitally important because your Life Vision should encompass all areas of your life. Without goals that encompass all of these areas then you will not ultimately be able to achieve all of your vision. If your Life

---

[41] Brian Buffini, *The Emigrant Edge*, (New York, NY: Howard Books, 2017), p. 200.

[42] John Maxwell, *Failing Forward*, (Nashville, TN: Thomas Nelson, Inc, 2000), p. 184.

[43] Brian P Moran & Michael Lennington, *The 12 Week Year*, (Hoboken, NJ: John Wiley & Sons, Inc, 2013), p. 95.

Vision is important to you, then you will formulate goals for each area of your life.

There are six life domains that I believe we all should have goals for. They follow the six life domains that I said were important to have in your Vision. These areas include spiritual, physical, relational, financial, professional, and personal. If they are important enough to have in your Vision then they should be important enough to formulate goals around.

I think that everyone has a deep desire to grow in their relationship with God, their Creator, Father, and Brother. Imagine for a second if you have a desire to go deeper with the Lord but don't know where to begin. Formulating a goal of "Starting March 1st, I will do a daily meditation every morning for 15 minutes." Just think of how much forming a goal like that will help you grow in the spiritual area of your life!

Not only are we spiritual beings, but we are physical beings as well. Our physical health and fitness are paramount for our own personal productivity and ability to thrive in life. We also cannot do much good in this world if we do not take care of ourselves physically. I see so many people who have all kinds of things that they want to achieve in their life, but they just cannot physically do them because they have not taken care of themselves physically.

I also believe that we need to have good relationships with our spouse, children, extended family and our closest friends. Setting goals for yourself relationally will greatly aid in the building up of those relationships most important to you. If you do not formulate goals that involve your relationships then they may end up not being relationships at all. I have found way too many individuals who said their marriage was important to them, but they never set goals to show that it was important. Tragically, many of those marriages ended in divorce.

Financial goals are where you want to be with your net worth so you can do more of the things you like to enjoy or to also give more away. Without developing concrete, specific financial goals...good luck, you may never see that financial dream come to fruition. As a Financial Advisor I have seen many people just fail to plan for their financial futures. I think the number one reason for this is because they fear that it may take a little work. Well, it does! However, it is just a little work.

Professional goals involve the place where we will spend most of our time, and so to not have goals there could be detrimental to your happiness. If you spend most of your time in the office and working to provide for your family, professional goals just make sense. Also, without professional goals you may just find that you are miserable most of your waking days. The reason for this is because most of us spend more time professionally than in any other life domain.

Finally, personal goals can hit on all of the areas. One personal goal I have is to travel with my wife Cyndi at least once a quarter. That personal goal filters into two other areas of my life; relational and financial. I can only go on a trip with my wife if I can financially afford it, so that financial goal will necessarily have to be met. Also, my wife will need to actually want to come with me on a trip, so I need to make sure that my relationship with her is thriving as well. That's where the relational goal fits in. Each area of your life is meant to build up, support, and be in service of the others. They all, working together, help the others stay where they need to be in order to thrive.

Goal-setting expert Michael Hyatt gives us two types of goals. "Both achievement and habit goals can help us design the future we want."[44] "Achievement goals are focused on one time accomplishments. Habit goals involve regular, ongoing activity, such as a daily meditation practice, a monthly coffee date with a friend, or walking each day after lunch."[45] This is excellent! An example of an achievement goal in the professional life domain may be to get 10 new clients by the end of the quarter. As far as the physical life domain, a habit goal may look like this: to work out 30 minutes a day, five times each week, for three months. Hyatt also gives helpful ideas on how to achieve the two types of goals. He talks about how a great idea for an achievement goal is to create deadlines. Having a goal that is time-keyed is vitally important for moving your own personal needle regarding the goal, especially a habit goal. Hyatt also lays out the necessity of trying to combine a "start date, habit frequency, time tracker, and a streak target."[46] He also has his Free To Focus Planner that helps to track all of these things for your habit goals. I have found it to be a very valuable tool.

[44] Michael Hyatt, *Your Best Year Ever,* (Grand Rapids, MI: Baker Books, 2018), p. 127.
[45] *Ibid.*, p. 128.
[46] *Ibid., p.* 129.

For most people who live in the United States, we are all very comfortable. I realize that we do have struggles but for the most part we are all living in a very comfortable society. Hyatt recognizes this and therefore provides us with some challenges when it comes to our goals. "For a goal to matter, it has to stretch us. That means it has to stand somewhere outside our comfort zone."[47] "The really important stuff of life happens outside your comfort zone. This is where the growth happens, where the solutions are, where fulfillment resides."[48] For a goal to be meaningful, its attainment should lie in the discomfort zone."[49] This goes back to what he said about how a goal needs to be risky. I challenge you to put your goals in the discomfort zone. Make the goal something that really stretches you, so that when you think about it you raise your eyebrows and say, "Whoa, I don't know about this one!" Make the goals as meaningful to you as possible, and then make them really stretch you. If you would like to lose 10 pounds but could really be helped by losing 25, then put that down instead.

Goals are about growing. A good goal causes us to grow and mature. That is because every goal is about the journey as much as and even more than the destination. Even if we don't hit every goal we set, which we won't, at least we will grow. At least we will get better. Let's say you put down a real stretch goal to lose 25 pounds in three months and you only lose 15. Isn't that better than where you were before? Or say your habit goal is to run 5 days a week for three

[47] *Ibid.,* p. 137.
[48] *Ibid.,* p. 138.
[49] *Ibid.,* p. 139.

months. Then you only run 3 days a week for that time. Are you not in better shape because you actually did get off of your rear end and get moving? Any progress is better than no progress at all. Forming goals is so critical for you to get to your own personal vision and will ultimately help you to live out your mission!

Work, Work, Work

This leads me to the importance of carrying out the actions that need to be done in order to achieve your goals. You have written the goals down. You have put down the action steps. You have also written down the possible obstacles that can arise and have made a plan of action ordered to attacking those obstacles. Now, you just need to go out there and do it! It's one thing to just write all of this stuff down. It's a completely different thing to actually get up off the couch and start acting. Now, to be honest with you, it is going to take some work, and the idea of taking the steps to achieve lofty and risky goals may be daunting, but the most important step here is to just start. Get some momentum going and it will begin to get easier day by day.

Brian Buffini reminds us, "A dream is not enough unless it is supported by a specific set of goals and the relentless hope needed to achieve them....Goals are the oxygen of dreams; without them, your dreams will stay just that—dreams."[50] Goals are the targets that you set to turn

---

[50] Brian Buffini, *The Emigrant Edge*, (New York, NY: Howard Books, 2017), p. 65.

your dreams into reality. That is encouragement for us to get moving on our goals. We have to be <u>relentless</u>, as Buffini says. Think about that for a minute. What does it mean to be relentless? Think about one thing that you wanted so badly that you just really, really went after it until you got it. That is what it means to be relentless. To never quit and to never stop, no matter what. Are your dreams worth being relentless for? Or are you going to sell yourself short?

In discussing successful people, Buffini says, "They know that their future is dependent on today's efforts, so even when they meet difficulty, they do not stop working toward their goal. They are relentless and dogged in their pursuit and never put off until tomorrow what they can do today."[51] This is the way of the Emigrant. "They don't just have good intentions—they are intentional in their approach to life and business."[52] Wow, are you kidding me? I think that really sums up the importance of being relentless. As he says, this is your future we are talking about. He uses the words *dogged* and *relentless* to get across the point that it takes a valiant effort on your part to achieve your goals, which will then lead you to accomplishing your vision.

Celebrate, Celebrate, Celebrate!

We all like a good celebration right? It is so important to remember to celebrate your successes. When you achieve a goal, make sure you do something good for yourself. For

---

[51] *Ibid.*, p. 122.
[52] *Ibid.*, p. 122.

each one of the goals I set for myself, I establish a reward for myself if I accomplish it. An example is that I have a habit goal of working out at least six times each week for a quarter. If I do that then my reward is a new pair of running shoes. I also have an achievement goal of paying off all of our debt. If I achieve that then the reward is a nice trip for Cyndi and I and we will pay cash for it. Without stipulating rewards and then following through with the rewards we can lose the motivation to achieve our goals.

Jon Maxwell says, "Point to success and celebrate. Acknowledge the successes and build on them."[53] I love that part of building on success. The more we achieve with our goals, the closer we will get to our ultimate vision and dreams. Plus, it's always fun to celebrate. Maybe your goal is to lose 50 pounds in a year. You do it, and then you treat yourself to the best chocolate cake ever made.

Maxwell also says, "Incentives, develop some, and when you achieve your goals, reward yourself."[54] The bottom line is celebrate, celebrate, celebrate!!!

Summary

I have obviously spent a lot of time writing on goals and how critical they are in helping you to achieve your dreams and vision. The bottom line is that goals are really that important! Without having them and without taking the actions to achieve them, we will forever be stuck in neu-

---

[53] Maxwell, *3 Things Successful People Do*, p. 76.
[54] Maxwell, *Failing Forward*, p. 173.

tral. Perhaps we will be alive and breathing, but not really going anywhere.

The ultimate reason that goals are set is *to help achieve your vision.* Goals need to be written down and are best if they are SMARTER Goals. Write down why they are important to you. Goals can be achievement oriented or habit oriented. They should cover all areas of your life. You also need a written plan for the obstacles that may sidetrack you from achieving your goals and specific steps to deal with them. Finally, when you achieve your goals, then don't ever forget to celebrate.

Hopefully by now you have come up with your Mission Statement as well as your Vision for your life. Now it is time to put together some goals toward your Vision.

You need to have a plan put in place that will include action steps that are specific, either daily or weekly, to move you forward. In the next Chapter we will cover this fourth pillar of success. One thing to keep in mind is that the actions you are taking with your goals are not only leading you to your Vision, but also following your *why* or your *Mission.* So, put this book down and put together your goals. Keep them simple, maybe between 10 to 12 for a year or 2 to 3 for a quarter. Write your goals down so you can truly thrive!

Pillar Four & Practice Four: Action Steps

n the previous Chapter I shared with you how Michael Lennington and Brian Moran talked about daily tactics to achieve your goals. They also shared with how these must be specific, measurable, time bound, and be actionable with assigned responsibilities. I also shared in the previous Chapter about how Ziglar talks about daily goals. I have heard Brian Buffini talk about the importance of having daily goals as well.

These tactics or daily goals are what I like to refer to as Action Steps. It all goes back to knowing that goals are vitally important to help you achieve your vision, but that does not go far enough. You must also have a written plan and action steps and a plan for dealing with things that will get in the way.

They are kind of like mini-goals, maybe that happen on a certain day or within a week. They are meant to be the intentional daily or weekly things that you are doing to get you closer to your goals and then eventually to your Vision.

I make sure that when I write down my goals that I also include my next actions that I must take to achieve my goals. My daughter, Emma, recently completed her Judges Clinic.

She is a gymnast and this clinic is the first time before they actually compete that they get judged on their routines. The judges then give them some helpful tips on what they need to work at to get better. Emma shared with me what her goals would be for the first meet, in terms of what her scores would be. I told her to write those down and then to write down some very specific actions that she needed to take to help her get the scores she was shooting for.

The important thing when it comes to goal setting is to make sure you are intentional in your daily actions to help you achieve your goals. Remember what I had told Emma when she told me her goals after her judges clinic? I told her she would have to write down action steps so she could achieve her goals. This is being intentional. Formulating and writing down your goals is one thing. Forming action steps is going above and beyond and putting those action steps in writing yourself will help you hold yourself accountable to achieve whatever goal you set for yourself.

In order to be successful in achieving our goals, vision, and dreams we must be willing to review our own progress. Michael Hyatt emphasizes, "It is important to have a regular goal review process. You can't just write goals and motivations. You have to review them and keep them top of mind."[55]

One can review every day, or once a year. I think both of these are important. A daily review is just something to do so you can properly put down for the next day the most important steps to move you forward. "The daily review

---

[55] Michael Hyatt, *Your Best Year Ever*, (Grand Rapids, MI: Baker Books, 2018), p. 214.

is designed to make that connection between goals and tasks."[56] This will help you to take the next best steps to achieve your goals. Hyatt expresses the importance of this review time so that we can keep moving forward. We need some time to decompress and think each day to remind ourselves what's really important. Some people take time every quarter and take time away from the office, home, and everything else for a morning to see where they are at and maybe establish some new goals. I do this and it has been very helpful to keep me on track.

A weekly review of your progress is something that I would encourage you to do. This is not something that will take a whole morning. A weekly review, even done diligently, can be done in 30 minutes. I got this idea from Hyatt as well and have implemented the Weekly Review into my goal planning. The weekly review focuses on three things. "The first part is to stay intellectually and emotionally connected to your motivations. The second part of the weekly review is a mini After Action Review. Review your progress. List your wins and your misses. The third and final part of the weekly review is to get a sense of what needs to be accomplished for the upcoming week."[57] After you assess what needs to be accomplished for the upcoming week, do not forget to write it down. These are the action steps to take that very next week.

Please, please do not leave this part out of doing regular reviews. It is critically important if you are going to achieve all of your dreams. Without those reviews you will get off

---

[56] *Ibid*, p. 216.
[57] *Ibid.*, pp. 216-217.

track and ultimately you will fail. Put these daily, weekly, quarterly, and annual reviews in your calendar. *What you put in your calendar will get done.*

I would also really emphasize taking five to ten minutes at the end of your work day to review your goals. In this particular quarter you may be focused only on one or two goals so this just won't take that long. The reason to do this is so you can plan up to three things you can do the very next day which I like to refer to as the Big 3 Rocks. The idea behind this is that if you were given large rocks, small rocks, pebbles, and sand and were told that it would all fit into a particular container, what would you put in first? The answer to the question is the larger rocks. If you put in the sand and pebbles in first then you would likely find the container may not be able to fit in the large rocks. If you put in the large rocks first, then the small rocks, followed by the pebbles, and sand then you could get it all in. Thus, with your To Do's each day, do your Big 3 Rocks first.

If you want to be successful in achieving your goals and life vision then you must have up to 3 Big Rocks each day. In essence, these are the next best Action Steps that you would take the next day to help you get closer to those goals and life vision. You may have 10 to do's the next day, but if you at least get done with those 3 Big Rocks then you can walk away saying you had a successful day even if that means some of the to do's that really are just pebbles have to be left for another day.

Let me give you an example of some good Action Steps on a day to day basis that you may put down to get you closer to your goals. These would be part of the Big 3

Rocks. Let's say that you have a goal to get 10 new clients or customers in the particular quarter you are in. One day you may have a specific Action Step to call 20 prospects to schedule meetings. The next day you may have the exact same Action Steps. The next day you may not have a few meetings scheduled so you may have an Action Step that says, assess the prospects needs and introduce the services we offer. The next day you may have Action Steps to set up closing interviews with the people you had just met with. Another Action Step could be to put together a presentation to help solve their problem with your product or service.

I hope that all makes sense. I also know that this seems so simple, but just like with goals, the fact is that if you do not write these things down then they will likely not get done. Action Steps really are just as important as goals in getting you closer to your life vision and to help you totally live out your mission in life.

Let me summarize this fourth pillar by once again laying out the steps for incorporating your Action Steps. You begin writing down your Action Steps in coordination with your goals. So, once you come up with your goals for the quarter or year, you should then go back under those goals and put down all of the action steps you can think of in order to achieve that goal. For instance, let's say you have a goal of losing 15 pounds this quarter. Your first action steps could be; call the local health club and schedule a time to learn what they offer, sign up for the membership, schedule three days per week in your calendar to go to the health club, download a fitness app, put a daily reminder to record your calories in the fitness app. Now, once you are on your way day after day and week after week in getting those actions done, you would then review daily and weekly the next best steps to help you achieve your goals. Write those next best action steps down for the next day or next week.

Build your momentum. That is probably the number one thing that Action Steps do. They really help you to build and maintain the momentum you need to be successful. It won't always be perfect, but that is not the point. The point is to be persistent!

There you have it! In this entire section we have defined what success is, as well as to provide the four pillars of success. We have looked at the importance of having a personal Mission Statement, Vision, Goals, and Action Steps. You are now well on your way to the journey of success. In the next section I will take you even further. I want you to be exceptional on your journey, and the two important things I think can assist you in becoming exceptional are accountability and coaching.

Becoming Exceptional On Your Journey

Practice Five: Accountability

When it comes to vision seeking and goal achieving, having quality accountability is important. You can classify accountability into two types: *self-accountability* and the *accountability of others*. I believe both are important, and anyone who is trying to reach their vision should have both types of accountability.

Let's start with that first type of accountability: Self-accountability. An individual who is trying to do great things by living out their mission, trying to be successful in seeing their vision come to fruition, and trying to achieve their own personal goals *must* hold themselves accountable. You cannot rely on others to just hold you accountable. You must hold yourself accountable if you want to achieve your dreams. I have tried to do this for as long as I can remember. I specifically remember doing it in high school Cross Country and Track. I had goals for each of these two sports and I would often reflect to see where I was at to see if I was making any progress on my goals. I tracked my workouts, the times I was running, and I even tracked how many days a week I got up in the morning for an early morning run. I have continued to reflect on where I am at in my career by tracking my numbers so that I can always push myself forward and give myself a good kick in the butt if needed.

There is a reason why I think that tracking your activity and results is so important, which is best summed up by Brian Moran and Michael Lennington when they talk about keeping score. Moran and Lennington say, "Measurement builds self-esteem and confidence because it documents progress and achievement...Effective measurement captures both lead and lag indicators that provide comprehensive feedback necessary for informed decision making. Knowing your numbers allows you to make intelligent decisions...Your results are created by your actions."[58] Notice that they don't say you should keep score so that you will recognize when you lose. No, they talk about how it will help you recognize your wins and how far along you have come. Keeping score is not meant to bring you down. It is meant to build you up and motivate you.

As part of my Weekly Review I take some time to get an overview of my numbers. In my business I have set out some very specific goals and every week I see where I am at with my numbers to make sure I am tracking so that I can achieve my goals. If I am not on track then I will know I need to make some adjustments on how I am running my business so that I have a better chance of achieving my goals.

Moran and Lennington also talk about the importance of self-accountability. In fact they call it "the only accountability that truly exists."[59] I don't know if I would go that far

---

[58] Brian P Moran & Michael Lennington, *The 12 Week Year*, (Hoboken, NJ: John Wiley & Sons, Inc, 2013), pp. 34-35.
[59] *Ibid.*, p. 47.

with it, but it definitely takes precedence over having others hold you accountable. Having others holding you accountable is important as we will see later, but your goals, your vision, your mission are just that, *yours*. They are not somebody else's, so naturally, you will be able to hold yourself accountable much better than someone else can because they are your dreams. Moran and Lennington also state, "In its purest form, accountability is simply taking ownership of one's actions and results."[60]

The reason why self-accountability is so important is because this really is the only accountability that can happen every day. Someone else may not always be with you to help you stay accountable. The great thing about self-accountability is that you are always with yourself. You can never be separated. You may have the greatest friends or the greatest co-workers and the greatest spouse, but that doesn't mean you can get them motivated enough every day to hold you accountable. Ultimately, they have to hold themselves accountable to their dreams, vision, and goals.

Moran and Lennington have already emphasized the importance of keeping score for ourselves. They go even further in stating, "Measurement drives the execution process."[61] They affirm, "Without measurement there is no way for you to know unequivocally if you are making progress."[62] Remember that we have a tendency to get caught up in our results, but Moran and Lennington suggest that it is also important to focus more on your actions each day rather

---

[60] *Ibid.,* p. 143.
[61] *Ibid.,* p. 122.
[62] *Ibid.,* p. 122.

than the results. "Remember, you have greater control over your actions than you do your outcomes...So the process is less about the end result and more about the daily actions."[63]

I believe that it is vitally important to track your goals. You should do this by measuring how you are doing. If you don't track your progress, then you are likely to veer off course and ultimately fail. As part of my Weekly Review I also take a look at the actions I have taken in the week to help me get closer to my goals. There are some weeks that are terrible and I have done hardly anything in terms of my actions to help me achieve my objectives. Moving to the next week I will be sure to write down more specific actions to move me forward.

Let's break down those two last quotes from Moran and Lennington. First and foremost measurement, tracking, and reflecting all help you to see where you are at and how much progress you are making. Without seeing progress there is a strong chance that you will give up on your goals. By tracking things you can see progress even if it's just a little and this will just create the momentum you need to keep going. Seeing a little progress is better than seeing no progress at all. It is also important to see what actions you have taken each day to make the progress. Maybe 75% of your actions have led you closer to your objective but 25% have not. You can then modify your actions to focus more on those that are taking you in the right direction and eliminate those actions that are not. Without measuring and tracking you are not able to do this. Again, holding yourself

---

[63] *Ibid.*, p. 122.

accountable is not meant to punish you, but it is meant to motivate you to go further.

Now that we have the idea of how important self-accountability is, we now can turn to accountability type number 2: Accountability of others. After we have self-accountability down then we can also utilize the accountability of others, and I do this regularly. Cyndi, my lovely bride, holds me accountable in all phases of my life. She helps me to be a better husband and father, but she also helps me to be the best Financial Advisor I can be. Her advice, input, and accountability are vital to my success. I also have my co-workers hold me accountable as I share with them what my goals are and then report to them where I am at. I will also do this with my closest friends. It is important to have a variety of people, and the most important thing is they have a vested interest in your success.

Rory Vaden says, "At a fundamental level, we need each other to motivate, empathize, push, challenge, and celebrate. We have the power to help each other change our lives."[64] I love how he describes accountability of others. It is all about helping one another to change our lives. This makes us all better which in essence will lead to better families, places of work, communities, and ultimately the world. He also says, "Create accountability in your life. Share your vision with someone who can encourage you, develop action plans with people who can help you, invest in your dream."[65] We

---

[64] Rory Vaden, *Take The Stairs,* (New York, NY: Penguin Group, Inc, 2012), p. 187.

[65] *Ibid.,* p. 189.

cannot do anything on our own. If we do things as a team we can be much more successful.

Brian Buffini also encourages having others hold us accountable. He says, "When you're working to achieve your goals, spending time with like-minded people who share similar values really is a no brainer."[66] Getting help like this "enhances your short- and long term goal achievement, helps you track your success, and improves your performance."[67] Again, it is all about not only helping you, but helping others. I choose to hang out with people who are driven like I am. By doing this we are able to hold one another accountable.

In order to make sure that you have both self-accountability and the accountability of others it is important to be consistent with a few things. First and foremost make sure you are reviewing your progress regularly. Keep score and take a brief look at that daily. Another really good practice to get into is a 30 minute weekly review. I would also encourage you each quarter to set aside about 90 minutes to do a Quarterly Review. Finally, set aside a morning or even a day annually to see what progress you have made. On this Annual Review come up with some new goals or maybe even adjust your vision. You may find there are some areas of your vision that are no longer applicable. I really love taking the time each year to do this Annual Review. It also allows me to reflect on my Mission to make sure I am truly living it.

---

[66] Brian Buffini, *The Emigrant Edge*, (New York, NY: Howard Books, 2017), p. 183.
[67] *Ibid.*, pp. 184-185.

When it comes to accountability of others I would suggest you have those informal meetings with those closest to you. Cyndi and I don't have a regular accountability meeting set up, but we do visit a lot and we especially do on our weekly date nights. With your closest friends maybe you can pick one or two that will be accountability partners and then you can share with each other your scores. It is a good idea to get these meetings scheduled and maybe shoot for once a month.

I have been blessed to be part of a Mastermind Group, which is a group of Financial Advisors located throughout the country. We visit about every other month and we share our scores with one another so we can each help one another achieve our vision and goals.

With people you work with I would encourage you to have regularly scheduled meetings with an agenda in place so you don't waste time. As a part of the meeting it would be important to share with each other your goals for that month, quarter, or year and then report your progress on them. If you are off target for some reason then a discussion can be had to help one another come up with solutions for how to get back on track. It really is all about helping one another.

Accountability is huge!! We were all made to thrive, and if we really want to do our part then we have to hold ourselves accountable, hold others accountable, and have others hold us accountable. In the next chapter I will be showing you a way to step up the accountability by using a coach. If you really want to excel on your journey to success then employing a coach will likely get you to where you want to go faster.

Practice Six: Coaching

Some of the greatest relationships that I have ever had in my life have been relationships with coaches. I look back fondly and remember specifically my first coach. He was my T-Ball Coach. All of the other boys on the team called him "Coach," but I called him "Dad." One of the gifts that my Dad and T-ball Coach had was the innate ability to encourage us boys. His enthusiasm and desire for us to be the very best little T-ball players was contagious. He was always able to get the very best out of us.

I remember one game that my Dad (Coach) was late for. I don't remember all of the details about the game, but I clearly remember that we were losing, not to mention the fact that we were not playing well. I also don't remember why my Dad was late, but I would guess it was due to him rushing straight from work. He finally arrived and from that moment until the end of the game everything changed. I can still hear all of those encouraging words that he built us up with, and we began to play much better as a team! I also remember that his presence changed us and our team dynamic. Man, he was a good T-ball coach! Our team of little, determined T-ballers came together, ended up coming back and even winning that game, and I remember how excited we were.

Now, that past story was from when I was 7 years old, but it is still so vivid in my mind today. The reason for this is the tremendous impact he had on us boys. Coaches have a tendency to have that significant of an impact. A really good, driven coach is remembered for years and years by those whom he coached. How many a professional athlete looks back fondly and tells stories about their high-school coach when giving credit and shout-outs for certain achievements. I think back to my own High School Cross Country and Track Coach, George O'Boyle. I have countless stories about him and the impact he has had on me and others. I have so many, in fact, that I have a book with many of those stories written across several pages. I have also been blessed the past several years to hire personal coaches to assist me in being the very best leader that I can be.

I am pretty sure that most of us have vivid memories of the coaches that we have had in the past or maybe even a great teacher or mentor. Because they have had such a significant impact on our lives I also often wonder why we stop having coaches. There seems to be some unwritten rule of society that once we are in our mid-20s, we no longer need any more help. How absurd this is! For some reason, we are all expected to just "have it all figured out" by a certain age, and if we don't then we missed the mark somehow. No! Coaching doesn't have to stop once you "grow up." There is always someone that knows and has experienced more life that would be willing to help you and push you to be the best that you can be in everything that you do. I'm 49 years old and I still have a coach! People aren't meant to go at life all by themselves without help. You are no exception! Coaching and having someone to walk with you as you strive to thrive in every area of life is something I believe in. I understand and know the importance of having a coach.

My first experience with a Life Coach or Personal Productivity Coach was with Larry Keiter. I originally met Larry and his family coming out of Mass at St. Mary's in the little town of Denton, Nebraska. We were new to the parish and he came right up to me and introduced himself and his family. Wow, what a blessing that was to meet them.

Seven years after meeting Larry I asked him if he would be willing to do some Strategic Planning and Leadership Development for my three business partners and me. Larry had recently taken a position at Ameritas Life Insurance Corp, and said he would love to do it, but was committed to his work at Ameritas. Because our firm had a strong relationship with Ameritas he made the decision to ask the CEO of Ameritas if he could help us. She was more than willing to loan him out to us! I was so happy about it.

Larry did a great job in helping us, and as part of the fee that we paid him he agreed to provide Leadership Development Coaching for a year for the four partners. This was invaluable to me, and he kept telling me that as Managing Partner I had a responsibility to do this type of coaching with those individuals who worked for us. That is really how I got my own personal start in coaching people. I give Larry a whole lot of credit from taking me from where I was at to a much better place. For me, personally, this was an absolute game-changer.

More recently, I have also utilized one-on-one coaching with Buffini & Co. I enjoyed my year of coaching with them because at the time I really needed assistance in maintaining balance in all the areas of my life. I had just recently sold my stock in my old firm and began my own firm. In order to be successful with my new firm I knew of the temptation to burn that midnight oil. Buffini and Co. really set me up for success in that first year.

I have also been blessed to be a part of Michael Hayatt and Company's Business Accelerator. This is a program of quarterly intensive days where I get together with other business leaders for assistance in learning how to run, operate, and scale a business. It is held under a group coaching format. Not only have I benefited from my coach, but also all of those others who are involved. There is a whole lot more involved with this program, but I just wanted to highlight the important role it has played in my business.

Many of you may also have a Financial Coach. This may be an individual who is a Registered Representative, Investment Advisor Representative, or Financial Advisor. This is a very good thing because you clearly see the need to have someone who is an expert in this area so you can get coaching and help to achieve your financial goals and dreams.

For many years I have also had a Spiritual Director. The best way to think of a Spiritual Director is it is someone who leads you in your journey of faith. They are there to coach you and give you ideas on how to grow closer to the Lord. The input I have received in Spiritual Direction has really laid the foundation for my growth in my faith.

Although, I have never personally had a Physical Fitness Coach, I do know the benefit that it can be to others. For 13 years I coached Cross Country and Track, and I believe a Physical Fitness Coach is similar in that they do everything they can do to get you into better shape physically. I have been a member of OrangeTheory for just over two years now, and in each class there is a coach. These 55 minute workouts are extremely intense and difficult. I would like to think I could do them entirely on my own, and that may be true, but there are days I know I could never make it through. The coaches at OrangeTheory do such a great job of getting you through the workouts.

I would like to give you five reasons why you might want to consider hiring either our coaching or another Personal Productivity Coach for your life.

A Coach Can Help You Write Your Mission Statement!

I have already discussed a Mission Statement in great detail. I hope that what I wrote in this book has helped you to write out a Mission Statement. However, your coach can get to know you and what is important to you. They can take a look at what you have written to make sure it really defines the why for you.

A Coach Can Help You Plan Your Life Vision!

It is so important to have a vision statement/life vision/strategic plan for your life. It can be a difficult process putting this all down on paper. A coach can assist you in examining what is really important to you and then putting together the vision of what that may look like.

A Coach Can Help You Formulate Goals!

I have also discussed in a previous chapter the importance of goals, and how goals help us to get closer to our Life Vision. Many of us struggle to not only put together our goals, but also to carry them out and follow through on them. A coach can do a great job helping and motivating us to achieve our goals so that we can achieve our vision. If we truly want to achieve our life vision then the formulation of and following through on goals is very important. A coach can help us to achieve these goals.

A Coach Pushes You!

I think this is the one thing that I have noticed more than anything else. A great coach is someone who really pushes you to excel to achieve your goals and your dreams. As part of pushing you they can hold you accountable to the goals that you set and have said were important for you to get you closer to your Life Vision. As we have already seen, accountability is so important and in the previous chapter I shared with ways others can keep you accountable. However, a coach is the best person you can use to keep you accountable. They are totally unbiased and they will really keep you on track. Family, friends and coworkers may be able to help, but sometimes they just let you off the hook. A great coach will also help you to come up with Action Steps to help you achieve your goals as well as to come up with new ones once you finish the first ones.

A Coach Helps You To Recognize Your Strengths!

This is vitally important. Unfortunately, most people are not even aware of what they are good at. I have been on retreats where we do what is called a Strength Bombardment. This is where each participant tells one participant a strength they see in them. Most people are so thankful for this because they never even realized what their strengths were. This is so tragic! How can we really thrive if we don't even know how to recognize our strengths. A coach is instrumental for us if we want to realize and actualize our strengths.

There are many other reasons that we should have a coach, but I think the five I have listed give good reasons for you to consider it. I want to emphasize that I have utilized coaching like this for the past 10 years, and I cannot emphasize how much it has benefitted me. It may be the biggest reason for my growth as an individual as well as in my business. This year I will personally pay about $13,000 for my coaching.

I have mentioned two different companies that I have used for coaching. I would encourage you to do some research either nationally or in your local community on what coaching is available and how it could be beneficial for you. You want to make sure you find a great fit!

I would be remiss if I did not share with you our coaching packages at Made2Thrive. I believe our coaching packages are extremely reasonable as far as cost and the value you get from it. We offer two different packages for people to utilize. You can find information on those two packages by going to https://made2thrive.live/made2thrive-coaching/. Let us help you to truly thrive in your life.

You have done such a great job in getting to this point of the book. I hope it has been helpful to you and your journey of success. I believe the first part of the book can help just about anyone to begin to thrive in their lives. The next section will be moving into ideas and tools that can specifically help you in your business and career. If you don't have a business or career then I do think there are some tools that you would still find helpful. Most people need help in all the domains of their life. If you are struggling in one area, then it can definitely be impacting others. The one area that almost always suffers is our career and business. I hope this next section can help you thrive in that area.

Tools For Business And Career

Practice Seven: Perfect Week

For years we have heard the term "work-life balance." For years I also thought that "work-life balance" meant that I needed to have an equal balance with the time that I am at work with the time that I am with my family. I have no idea why I ever thought that because, if you really think about it, that is not even possible. Let's look at the numbers. There are only 168 hours in a week. If you try to get 8 hours of sleep each night then that takes up one-third of your week, or 56 hours. If you are in the midst of your career then you likely work around 40 to 50 hours each week. Well, that would seem to leave you with another 52 hours for your family, correct? No, probably not. You have to have some time for yourself as well to work on your spiritual, emotional, and physical well-being. That could take another 10 to 20 hours per week. Then there is time for friends, community involvement, working on your finances, and on, and on, and on. This idea of "work-life balance" being an equal amount of time between work and family just isn't correct or realistic.

I like to define work-life balance as spending time on those things that you need to do to follow your mission and move you to your vision, when they need to be done. For many people with a career this would mean that when you are working you are totally focused at work and giving your best there. When you are with your spouse and children then you are totally in tune with them. When you are with friends, you are not allowing yourself to be distracted by work. When you are at your volunteer opportunities you are also totally engaged in that. Work-life balance means being totally focused on the aspect or area of your life that you are participating in during that moment. It means that in whatever domain of your life vision that you are in at any given moment, you are totally focused on excelling at it. There are seasons in life when that means working a little more. There are also seasons in life where your time is spent much more with family, such as a vacation or family mission trip.

In order to get the proper work-life balance I think it is very important to try and put together your perfect week. Note, not every week will be perfect, and quite honestly most won't be. However, that doesn't mean you should not strive to have the perfect week. Just because it won't be perfect every time doesn't mean to not try at all. Dave Ramsey says, "Managing time is the same; you will either tell your day what to do or you will wonder where your day went."[68] He further says, "...when you work a daily plan in pursuit of your written goals that flow from your mission statement born of your vision for living your dreams, you are ener-

[68] Dave Ramsey, *Entreleadership*, (New York, NY: Harper Books, 2011), p. 44.

gized after a tough long day."[69] I think that sums it up pretty well. Every day should be in pursuit of what is important to you, which flows from your mission in life and lead you to your vision and dreams.

I have found several books that talk a lot about scheduling your week. I have spent hours pouring through these books so I could become the most efficient person I can possibly be. One book I really enjoyed is *The One Thing*, by Gary Keller & Jay Papasan. Their book really talks about taking on that one thing that is most important, and if you are to be successful you must block your time off for that one thing. They also talk about the necessity of blocking out your planning time as well as your maker time. The maker time is the time you spend in moving your business forward and growing it. As a Financial Advisor this would mean meeting with clients in reviews as well as in helping them in their planning. I then need to make sure I am giving them the suggestions they need to help them achieve their financial goals. Keller and Papasan finally discuss the importance of blocking out your meeting times.[70] This means internal meetings you have with staff, so that everyone knows when the meeting is going to be so they can all be prepared.

I believe that if you want to be successful and achieve your goals then you have to make sure they are scheduled. Schedule tasks or to-do lists that will move you closer to your goals. If you need to schedule time blocks to focus

---

[69] *Ibid, p. 45.*
[70] Gary Keller & Jay Papasan, *The One Thing*, (Austin, TX Bard Press, 2013), Ch. 15.

on those important tasks then make sure you do so. I can often go week after week being consistent in building in time blocks to make sure I am doing those tasks that will get me closer to my objective. But then out of the blue I will have a Sunday afternoon where I think I have it all figured out and then I won't bother to do the time blocks for the coming week. This "I've got it all figured out" attitude is toxic to success and just sets me back. It is also important to create routines that will lead you closer to your goals. Having routines is also a great idea because it will help us to achieve those objectives. One routine I have every Sunday is I review my calendar for the upcoming week and then I schedule in my work outs for the week as well as the times I am going to set aside for prayer.

It is also so important to make sure you are scheduling in times to be down and away from work. Recovery is so important. I coached Track and Cross Country for 13 years and one of the hardest things that I had to do was to get my very best runners to take an easy day. They were so determined to be the best that they just wanted to go harder and harder and harder and always push themselves. If they continually did that then they would just physically break down. They needed at least one day a week for recovery. The same goes for us with our goals. If we are just always pushing and pushing and pushing then we will get worn down and it will prevent us from having the energy to accomplish our goals.

So many people have goals, but they don't do anything about them. Working towards those goals is not part of their regular routine. If we want to achieve them then they need to be top of the mind to us all the time. That is why they should be scheduled, and we should be building in routines to achieve them. In regard to my physical goals I have built in some routine with a workout schedule so I can be sure to achieve my physical goals.

Brian Moran and Michael Lennington also express similar sentiments when they say, "To realize your potential, you must learn to be more mindful about how you spend your time...organize your life around your priorities and consciously choose those activities that align with your goals and vision."[71] They believe that creating time blocks is a great way to focus on how to be more mindful with how you spend your time. "Block out regular time each week dedicated to your strategically important tasks...There are three primary components:

> Strategic block is a three-hour block of uninterrupted time that is scheduled into each week. You focus on strategic money-making activities. Buffer blocks are designed to deal with all of the unplanned and low-value activities. A breakout block is at least three-hours and spent on things other than work."[72]

I guess the way that may look for a Financial Advisor is maybe to start the first 30 minutes in Buffer Block mode,

---

[71] Brian P Moran & Michael Lennington, *The 12 Week Year*, (Hoboken, NJ: John Wiley & Sons, Inc, 2013), p. 40.
[72] *Ibid,* pp. 41-42.

checking emails or returning phone calls, then maybe you would have two client meetings for three hours, followed by a lunch break or maybe a work out and lunch. Then you come back in the office with some more buffer time checking emails and returning phone calls. Then finish up your work day with another 3 hours of client meetings. The evening would be your breakout block where you would spend time with family and friends.

Moran and Lennington also say, "Effective time use can be the difference between the mediocre and a great performance...The choices that you make on how you spend your time, ultimately create your results in life."[73] "To become great, you must choose to allocate your time to your greatest opportunities...To be great, you will need to live with intention."[74]

Intention is huge here. I have found that as I have structured and designed each of my weeks around my vision and goals that I have been much more intentional with doing what is important to me. I cannot waste time surfing the web and social media if I am going to accomplish my vision and goals. Also, if I am wasting my time then I am not doing anything that is fulfilling or giving me joy. When I am intentional about scheduling my week I accomplish great things.

Being intentional is simply a choice we have to make. Looking back on my own running career as well as on the careers of the student-athletes I coached, I can see a big difference between those who were intentional and those who

---

[73] *Ibid*, p. 129.
[74] *Ibid,* p. 131.

were not. If you wanted to be excellent during the season then you had to make sure you were training in the off season. If you were not intentional about it then there was no way you would be able to achieve your goals as a runner.

I also really enjoyed Greg McKeown's book, *Essentialism*. He says, "The reality is, saying yes to any opportunity by definition requires saying no to several others."[75] What does that mean? Heck, it means that if you say yes to golf for six hours, three days a week, then you would be saying no to your work, family, and other things 18 hours a week. Now, I am not criticizing people who play golf. I like golf and will get out several times each year. Hopefully, I will at least play with friends. One of the reasons that I do not play often is because it is not something I do with my family. If I did, then maybe I would golf more, because it can be a great way to spend time with family.

McKeown also talks about Jeff Weiner, the CEO of LinkedIn. He schedules in his workday up to two hours each day of blank space in 30 minute increments. That way he can take the time each day to process and think about his work and the meetings he has been having. This allows him to think about the future of the business and the vision for the future. It also allows him to shift between problem-solving mode and the coaching mode expected of him as a leader.[76]

This is a great example that Weiner provides to us. If we don't schedule in this important time to work and process

---

[75] Greg McKeown, *Essentialism*, (New York, NY: Crown Business, 2014), p. 52.
[76] *Ibid,* p. 69.

what we have been doing then we will become frustrated. If we allow ourselves to reflect on what we have done, we can take a bit of time to celebrate some wins.

McKeown also talks about the importance of setting boundaries with others, which can include your superiors and partners. It can also be for those who report directly to you. If boundaries are not set with these people then they will feel like they can just come in and interrupt your day whenever is convenient for them. I really struggled with this throughout my career. I always felt like I should have an Open Door Policy. However, if my door is always open then it leads to more interruptions on things that may or may not be urgent or important. I value my closed door because when it is closed it is then that I am working on something important or urgent. McKeown says, "If you want weekends off then set that boundary and don't ever cross it. If you don't set boundaries then someone else will set them for you. If you don't set boundaries then you will become spread so thin that getting anything done will become impossible."[77]

There are so many demands on each of our days. At one time in my life I was the type of person who would say yes to anyone or anything that was asked from me. I have been that way because I am a people-pleaser. Just look at my mission statement and you can tell that I have a real desire to help people. Here is the problem with saying yes to everything. The truth is you can't do that. Every time I would say yes to a request it meant I was also saying no to something else. This usually meant I was saying no to my wife or my

---

[77] *Ibid,* p. 166.

children. Early in my career I would meet with a prospect or client whenever they could. If that meant I was working three or four nights each week then I would do it. What did that mean for my family? Yep, three or four nights each week where I was not at home. How in the world could I be a good husband and father trying to maintain that schedule? Over time I began to realize that I really needed to schedule those things that are truly important to me.

One very important thing to me is to take a weekly date night with my wife Cyndi. When you have six kids who are involved in many activities, a business to run, as well as wanting to work out five to six days a week it can be very difficult to find time for a weekly date with your spouse. Well, this time with your spouse is vitally important so you have to schedule it. We don't have to do this quite as much now that we have older kids who can help watch younger kids as well as transport younger kids. However, Cyndi and I used to visit early each week to see when we could take a date night. We would then both make sure it was on our calendars.

In John Maxwell's book <u>Today Matters</u>, he talks about the importance of understanding what is important to us or our priorities. He gives five reasons for this:

1. Time is our most precious commodity.
2. We cannot change time, only our priorities.
3. We cannot do everything. You can have anything you want, but you cannot have everything you want. You have to choose.

4. We choose our life by how we spend our time.
5. Priorities help us to choose wisely.[78]

He goes on to further say, "Prioritize your life and give focus and energy to those things that give you the highest return."[79] Those things that give you your highest return are going to be the things that help get you closer to your vision. They will be the things that get you closer to your goals. My guess is that checking Facebook and Twitter are not giving you your highest return, but a weekly date night with your spouse and having 10 to 15 meetings with clients will.

Maxwell gives us three questions to consider when trying to figure out how to make a decision based upon our priorities. They are:

1. What is required of me?
2. What gives me the greatest return?
3. What gives me the greatest reward?[80]

Those are three very powerful questions. I already weighed in on the greatest return, but how you decide should also be determined by what will give you the greatest reward. You can think of reward in financial terms, but it could also be just how it makes you feel. Spending time with Cyndi is much more rewarding to me than surfing the web. Then you also have that first question. What is actually required of you? If the amount of time, work, and energy is

[78] John Maxwell, *Today Matters*, (New York, NY: Time Warner Book Group, 2004), pp. 66-68.
[79] *Ibid*, p. 69.
[80] *Ibid*, p. 71.

just too great to sacrifice other very worthwhile things then maybe you should just let it go.

To be the very best you can be and to really thrive then when trying to figure out where to spend your time remember to stay where you are strong. What are you good at that few people can do? What gets you jacked up? This is where you should spend your time. There are so many minutes in each day, and we should be spending those minutes on the things that we are really good at as well as those things that really drive us. We should spend our time on things that will take us closer to our vision.

Maxwell also talks about the importance of living each and every day by your priorities. <u>You can't just leave it all to chance</u>. You have to schedule your day and be intentional with your time. He gives five things to keep in mind when it comes to living each and every day by our priorities:

1. Evaluate priorities daily.
2. Plan your time carefully.
3. Follow your plan.
4. Delegate whenever possible.
5. Invest in the right people daily.[81]

Every one of these five points is so important. Every day I look at my calendar and I determine what are the most important things that I must do. Hopefully, most of these things are things that I am not only very good at but also enjoy immensely. In my work life it is meetings with clients. I very much enjoy each and every meeting. It gives me the

---

[81] *Ibid,* pp. 73-77.

opportunity to get to know them better but also to truly help them. That just jacks me up! Each time I have meetings with clients it is definitely one of the most important parts of my day.

You also have to plan accordingly. I make sure that in my calendar I give enough time for each meeting I have with a client. I don't ever want it to appear that I am rushing through the meeting just to get to another one. If I think I am going to need 1.5 hours to give me enough time to interact with that client then I might schedule it for two hours just in case.

Maxwell's third point of following your plan is also vital. I cannot tell you how many times I have not done that. Those are also the days where I really don't look at my calendar or the high value tasks that I must do. I then will end up wasting time on stupid things like social media or news that is just not important. Then because I did that I miss my work out or end up working late and then cannot spend time with my family. I get so frustrated when this happens, but we are all human, and that's when I take a breath and make a new start the next day remembering my priorities.

I will spend more time on delegation a little bit later in this book. I just want to state that it is impossible to do everything. Even if you try to do everything you will probably end up doing much of it badly. This is why it is so important to stay within those areas you are best at as well as passionate about. Delegate the other things. I used to think I could do any of my tasks better than anyone else. Talk about pride. I now realize that I am not good at a whole lot of things, and there are people out there who are really good and passionate about things that I am weak at and don't even enjoy.

Maxwell's last point here is simply investing in the right people. It takes a lot of thought to figure out who that is. For me, it is Cyndi and my children. They are my life, and they make me a better man, and I know I make them better too. I also have to invest very heavily in my clients. When you have hundreds of clients that can be difficult, but if that is the case then it is important to surround yourself with a great team who can help you. Who are the other people in your life that you need to invest in? Maybe it is a friend, colleague, or family member. What relationships will give you the greatest reward and return, not necessarily for yourself but for the other person?

By far my favorite individual in terms of personal productivity is Michael Hyatt. He is the former CEO of Thomas Nelson Publishers. He stepped down from that position after blogging on leadership and personal productivity for several years. He started his company Michael Hyatt & Co. Over the last few years his company has offered an online course called *Free To Focus*.[82] I have taken this course twice, and it has been a total game changer and life saver for me. It has helped me to become a better husband and father, financial advisor, and all around great guy. I want to share with you a few highlights from this course, but I also want to encourage all of you reading this to take the course and have your team take the course as well.

Hyatt refers to the four different quadrants that we have in our life. I want to focus on two of them here. One quad-

---

[82] https://freetofocus.com

rant is for things in our life that are both important and urgent. Another quadrant that we should focus on are those things that are important but not urgent. Why should we spend our time in those two quadrants? It's pretty simple, actually: both are important! We have a tendency to spend time on things that are not important and therefore we have a tendency to just waste our days away. Hyatt explains in the course that these two quadrants are so important because they deal in areas of importance. These quadrants should be scheduled into your day. He actually says we should schedule an appointment for them because these "represent non-discretionary time." He also says, "these commitments have to be filled at a specific time on a specific day."[83]

For me something in the Important and Not Urgent quadrant might be my client meetings. They are typically never urgent unless the client has a very urgent request. Because my client meetings are important I always have a certain amount of time slots allocated for client meetings each week. Another important but not urgent thing for me is time with Cyndi. In fact it is very, very important so I will make sure I get a weekly date on the schedule with her. I also try to do this with each of my six children. An important and urgent thing could be a client that needs to take money out of an account and needs to best determine which account to take it out of. This is likely time sensitive, so I will have my assistant call and schedule a time I can call them back so all of my focus is on helping them. Something else that is both important and urgent is getting Sam to his baseball game or practice on time. If I have to do this on

---

[83] *Ibid.*, Lesson 7.

a particular night, then you better believe I have it on my calendar because this is very important and it is urgent that I get him there.

Lesson Eight of the Free To Focus Course was an absolute game changer for me.[84] Hyatt shares three activity categories. By breaking down your days according to these three activity categories it will make you much more productive than you are now. It took me well over a year until I fully began doing this, but since I finally made this change I have seen my personal productivity literally go straight up.

There are front stage activities which are activities where you are performing your job. As I stated earlier Moran and Lennington refer to this time as Strategic Blocks. This could be meeting with clients or vendors. In essence these are the things you do to actually make money. Front stage activities are where you should be spending a significant amount of your time. It may not be the bulk of your time, but it is your most important time. For me, this really is my time in front of clients in a meeting or visiting with them on the phone or exchanging emails.

Category two activities are what Hyatt calls "backstage activities." Moran and Lennington referred to these as the Buffer Blocks. These are all the activities that happen behind the scenes. These activities are what make your front stage possible. Hyatt says, "Five types of backstage work would include preparation, in which you prepare for your role on stage. Delegation, which is enrolling others and helping you prepare. Coordination, which involves meeting with your team to coordinate the work. Clean up is where you

---

[84] *Ibid,* Lesson 8

clean up after the performances. Type five is development. This type of work involves developing new systems that will enhance or streamline your performances."[85]

I want to touch just a bit more on these backstage activities. Preparation is the one I find most valuable. It would be like taking the time to memorize lines of a play that you are in. If you don't memorize the lines then you will never be able to go on stage for the performance. I used to delegate quite a bit of my appointment preparation, and I still do to some extent, but I see appointment preparation as the equivalent of memorizing lines. If I don't do this part well then I will not be able to get onstage for the "performance" with my clients.

On my back stage days I do take time to think about some of the activities that I am doing that really should be delegated to my assistant who could do those activities better than myself. A couple of these activities are taking calls from clients or scheduling meetings with clients. I have found that if I am doing these two activities, it is very easy for me to spend my whole day on the phone. When I call my clients for any reason those calls can be 10 to 15 minutes in length, whereas when my assistant makes the calls they are much shorter. I would much rather spend those minutes in front of my clients than on the phone with them.

The last one of those backstage or buffer block activities I want to touch more on is development. The reason this is a backstage activity is because I cannot be doing this while in front of my clients. I will only do this activity on those days where I can really take the time to focus on

---

[85] *Ibid*

developing these new systems that will make me a better Financial Advisor.

What Moran and Lennington refer to as Breakthrough Blocks, Hyatt refers to as "offstage activities." This is time away from work whether it's Strategic Blocks or Buffer Blocks. It is time dedicated to rejuvenation. For me this is always Saturdays and Sundays, and sometimes it will be on a Monday or Friday as well or at least for some of those days. When I first started my career I would work 60 hours each week, and then when I wasn't working I was still "kind of" working. It was hard for me to have downtime, and that is just exhausting. Time away from work is vitally important if you want to be able to maintain the energy to be the best when you are truly at work.

Overall, I do try to categorize each of my days. I will lay out my perfect week just a bit later in this chapter, but for me my strategic blocks or frontstage Days are Tuesdays, Wednesdays, and Thursdays. These are days when I am out front meeting with my clients or prospects, vendor partners, or board meetings. Mondays and Fridays are typically when I am using my buffer blocks or backstage. However, it is very common on these two days to have some offstage Time too. In fact most of Friday is offstage, but I do look to allocate time to backstage work on Fridays. I will often finalize my appointment prep for next week's appointments on a Friday. I will also have calls with vendor partners or other work related items, but not usually with clients. Finally, Saturdays and Sundays are almost exclusively breakthrough blocks or Offstage. I try to avoid doing any career work on those two days.

I also want to share with you some final thoughts and ideas on setting up a Perfect Week for yourself. I believe it is vitally important that you come up with a Perfect Week. You can do this one of two ways. Either open up a Google Calendar and fill it in this way or just use a paper calendar. Really take the time to think what you want your Perfect Week to look like and then get it on paper or that Google Calendar. I always kind of had my plan in my head, but never wrote it down on paper. It is amazing how much you can change your life by just doing this one thing. As so many great authors have shown us in this chapter, it is important to put on your calendar those things that are most important to you.

One final thought on Hyatt's course. He is a big believer in batching your days so you will work on certain items at a certain time of the day so you are not distracted by other things during that time. I believe the reason for this is to build up a routine and to be consistent.

I want to lay out to you my perfect week. This is not necessarily how you should lay out your week. In fact, your perfect week may look nothing like my perfect week. My assistant is very aware of what my perfect week looks like. My family is pretty familiar with my perfect week as well. The reason they are familiar with it is because they will know when their husband or dad is available for them. You will notice that it is often. It has not always been this way. In the past, it was very common for me to have three to four evenings taken up by my career. That is no longer the case. All of my research that I have done on personal productivity shows that putting into your calendar what is important to you is the most effective way to make sure you spend time on the things that are important to you.

I want to encourage you to share your Perfect Week with your staff, your family, and all of your closest colleagues. It is important to share that with them so they know how you best work as well what is most important to you.

I do have my whole perfect week actually written out in a weekly calendar. That way I can review it every few weeks to make sure I am sticking to it or modify it if that would be best for me. To make things simple for this book I am only going to provide a summary of what my perfect week looks like. Here it is:

Off Stage   Day Sunday- Sunday Mass,
                     Family and Friends, Work Out

Back Stage   Day Monday
   6:00 - 6:30   Morning Prayer Time
   6:30 - 7:30   Get Ready For The Day
   8:15 - 9:00   Daily Mass
   9:00 - 9:30   Team Meeting
   9:45 - 10:45   Orange Theory Work Out
   1:00 - 4:00   Family Time, Emails and Return Phone
                     Calls, Vendor Meetings
   4:00 - 8:30   Family Time
   8:45 - 9:45   Whiskey and The Word Men's Group

Front Stage   Days Tuesday, Wednesday,
                     and Thursday
   6:00 - 6:30   Morning Prayer Time

6:30 - 7:30	Get Ready For The Day
8:15 - 8:45	Daily Mass
9:00 - 10:00	Client Meeting
10:00 - 10:45	Emails, Correspondence and Phone Calls, Apt Prep
11:00 - 12:00	Client Meeting
12:00 - 12:45	Lunch and Apt Prep
1:00 - 2:00	Client Meeting
2:00 - 2:45	Emails, Correspondence and Phone Calls, Apt Prep
3:00 - 4:00	Client Meeting
4:00 - 5:30	Run or Work Out
5:30	Family

Back Stage	Day Friday
6 - 6:30	Morning Prayer Time
6:30 - 7:00	Get Ready for The Day
7:30 - 8:00	Daily Mass
8:30 - 9:30	Orange Theory Fitness Workout
11:30 - 12:30	Sam to Pius
12:30 - 5:00	Household Chores, Work Emails, Read, Relax, Joseph Time, Work Calls
5:00	Family and Friends

| Off Stage | Day Saturday - Work Out, Family and Friends and Daily Mass |

It is really that simple. I have put down all of those things that are important to me. I hope you can see clearly how important my family is for me. I also hope you can see how important my faith is for me. You should also see how important it is for me to be physically fit. I have those things in my calendar. Also, I have 12 client meetings each week and only on three days. I realize that some Advisors have more client meetings than that, but there are a whole lot that have less than 8. My first Manager told me I should strive to have two a day, five days a week. That would only be 10, so I feel pretty good about 12. Also, I find that if I have that many appointments each week that I am easily able to achieve my business goals each year.

Ultimately, you have to determine what is important to you and then schedule out your perfect week and share it with others. Your calendar should only show those things that are important to you.

Now, is every week for me a perfect week? Of course not, who do you think I am kidding? I do strive to make each one of my weeks look like I have laid out for you, but rarely are the weeks like this. I have kids, and let me tell you their activities have a way to get in the way of a perfect week, and I would not have it any other way. Currently, Emma is in gymnastics so in the early part of the year I am doing some traveling with her during competition season. When Sam is playing baseball from March through the end of July I try to be at every game so that may mean that those weeks I have maybe 9 or 10 appointments because I may be leaving the office by 2:30 or 3 to get him to where he needs to be.

The important thing to remember about putting together a perfect week is that you should be the one to design it, not someone else. It's your week, not someone else's. Also, if adjustments need to be made because of things that come up, such as kids' activities, then you should be the one to determine the changes. Don't let someone else dictate to you what you are going to change. I used to do this, and it would drive me absolutely crazy and also made me unhappy. I am much happier when I am able to make my own decisions about what is important to me in terms of scheduling my time.

I want you to take some time now to put together your perfect week. If you want to thrive then this is a step you must make!

Practice Eight: Strengths

n order to achieve your vision and goals and to be truly living according to your mission statement, it is very important to be working each day within your strengths. What are you really good at? The answer to this question can be answered a number of ways, but it is important to answer it honestly. You will never be able to achieve your vision if you are not operating within your strengths. In Michael Hyatt's "Free To Focus" course he refers to working within your desire zone. Hyatt says, "This is the zone where you are passionate and proficient at something. This is true north for you and your top strengths. These tasks allow you to experience true freedom. True productivity is about doing more of what is in your desire zone and less of everything else."[86]

I couldn't agree more with Hyatt on the above point. When you are both passionate and proficient at something and you can spend the majority of your time doing that, then you are truly free. This is what I think people mean when they say that they never feel like they are going to work. You literally love it that much that it doesn't even feel

---

[86] https://freetofocus.com

like work. You almost feel like you could do that all day long. So it is very important to find out what you are both passionate and proficient at, and then focus on that.

In my experience, most people are not aware of what their strengths are. They may enjoy certain things, but they don't really know what they are proficient at. So, how do you go about discovering this? I encourage you to ask others what they think your strengths are. You may be surprised by what they say, and it can be very helpful to you. Another thing you could do is to take the "Strengths Finder" test with Gallup. This has really helped me to focus more on what my strengths are. Just Google "Strengths Finder" and you will find it. There is a small cost to go through this process, but I think it is well worth it.

For many years, I have directed a retreat for high school students. One part of the retreat is called Strength Bombardment. Each table of students and leaders goes around one-by-one sharing one strength or gift they see in each other. The only response the individual being praised can say back to each person is thank you. The reason for this is that we have a tendency to want to dismiss what others will say about us when they are pointing out a good quality. Instead, we should accept it. I suggest that if you work with a team of people to do some sort of a Strength Bombardment with your team members. The best people to help us are often those we are closest to as well as work with. I helped lead this at a company retreat for a non-profit organization where I was the President of the Board. It was the most beneficial part of their day-long retreat.

There are many things that I enjoy, and there are some things that I am proficient at. To be truly productive and to help me achieve my vision I have to combine these two. I love playing baseball, basketball, and football. However, I am just okay, and I am definitely not proficient in any of them. I am pretty proficient with math, but I don't want to be doing math all day long. It is definitely not something that excites me. The key to being successful is to find those things that we are both passionate and proficient at. Should I become the stat guy for a basketball team? No, I think I will pass on that offer!

Know your strengths. Once you know them you can then play to and leverage your strengths. Brian Buffini says, "The most successful people find out what their strengths are, match them with something they enjoy doing, and then do it."[87] This is similar to what Hyatt says about being both proficient and passionate at something. One thing that I am both proficient and passionate at is meeting and helping people. I am not necessarily an extrovert. I actually like to be by myself and would prefer that to being in a big crowd of other people. However, I love being with a small group of people. So, in my career, I have the most success when I am meeting with clients and prospects and helping them. If I can spend more time doing this and less on everything else, then I will be truly free and will be able to be successful.

The more you work in the areas that you really enjoy and are also very good at, the more you will enjoy what you do. If you are in a job where you are not very good at

---

[87] Brian Buffini, *The Emigrant Edge* (New York, NY: Howard Books, 2017), p. 204.

what you do, and you hate what you are doing, then this would be the worst situation for you. John Maxwell says, "Your strengths are the way to fulfill your why. Every time you use your strengths to live out your why, you build on your strength and increase your why."[88] As a reminder, your why is your mission. My mission is to assist in improving the lives of others by serving them with great passion. This is my why. If one of my strengths was doing back office activities, then I could fulfill my why by doing back office activities, but this is not my strength. My strength is sitting down and listening to what people want and then coming up with a plan to help them achieve that objective. This is where I need to spend most of my time. I have to work in areas that are my strengths so that I can most effectively fulfill my why.

I want to encourage you to stay in your strengths zone. Focus on the areas that you do really well. The more you are in your strength zone, the more productive you will be, and you are more likely to reach your potential. It is also extremely difficult to reach your potential if you spend most of your days in areas that you are weak in. My sister, Liesa Kasparek, is a Senior Project Manager for Ameritas Life Insurance Corp. She manages projects that typically have a technological component to them. She works with the end user to determine scope and budget for what they need, doing all the planning, and getting the resources to do the work. She also monitors the execution of the work being done. She compares it to being a building contrac-

---

[88] John Maxwell, *Intentional Living* (New York, NY: Hachette Book Group, 2017), p. 83.

tor working with a couple that is building a house. She helps Ameritas to fulfill their mission of fulfilling life by using her strengths. Although I can do what she can do, it is not something I am gifted at, so that is why she can help Ameritas fulfill their mission in that way, and I cannot.

I want to encourage you to understand that in order to truly thrive in your life, you will have to work within your strength zone. If you are trying to do everything, then you will not be successful in anything. Allow others to use their strengths, and focus on using yours. Working together as a team will lead to success and will lead you to truly thrive.

As we continue through this section of the book we will be taking a look at other aspects or tools to help you more effectively in your career. The next couple of chapters will assist you by allowing you to focus much more on your strengths. I will share with you the value of using a Client Relationship Management System as well as the importance of delegating properly so you can focus mostly on your areas of strength. The key with this is making sure you have the right people on your team!

Practice Nine: Client Relationship Management

t was October 2003, and I was having lunch with my good friend, Doug Pfeifer. Doug is also a Financial Advisor, and since he is a few years older than me, he has a bit more experience at it than I do. I have even told my wife Cyndi that if I die I would want to have her meet with Doug about the possibility of him managing her money. I have a lot of respect for Doug and how he runs his business and works with clients.

On that particular day, Doug was visiting with me about Gorilla Marketing. I had no idea what that meant, so he went into a little bit of detail explaining it. He said it really means just constantly staying in front of your clients and building processes and systems to do that. I asked him why that was so important, and he told me that if you take care of your clients it is easier to keep them rather than going out and finding new clients, and that the best source of new business was current clients rather than new ones. That seemed to make sense, so I inquired even further.

In response to my question about how do I go about staying in front of my clients, he asked me a question.

He asked if I had a CRM. I had absolutely no idea what he was talking about, so I asked him what in the world a CRM was. He said it was a Client Relationship Manager. I think I must have said something like I had not hired one of those yet, and he just laughed at me. He then explained it was a software program that helps to keep track of your clients' contact information, notes, and schedule for staying in front of them.

I had to think for a few minutes before we went on with the conversation. It seemed to me that I was using a CRM, but that it was not able to do everything that he said it should. So, I told Doug that yes, indeed, I did have a CRM called Broker's Ally. He then asked me if it was web-based and that just further confused me. What did he mean by web-based? Yes, I knew that he meant the internet and that "web-based" was not something a spider had created! However, I had very little understanding of what a CRM could do, and even less of an understanding of how it could go through the internet. After the meeting I was anxious to get back to my office to figure out exactly what Broker's Ally was and how it worked.

At that time, Broker's Ally was just a DOS-based system. I bet most of you reading this book don't even know what that means! That is how old-school it was. DOS was a computer operating system that was very inefficient and cumbersome to work with. Hey, at least I had something similar to what Doug was using, and I wanted to be a better Financial Advisor than him. I really didn't have a lot of extra money, so I thought I would just make the best of it with what I had. I would start utilizing this CRM on the old archaic DOS version and then do some research to see if there was a Windows-based version or even a web-based version. After a few months I was able to switch to the Windows version as they still did not have a web-based version.

I want to fast forward this story just a week or two to October 17, 2003. Cyndi was all of nine months pregnant with our son Sam. Her mother was in town from Colorado to help us with the three older kids as Cyndi would go into labor. Well, that night when I got home from the office she told me she thought she was in labor. It was pretty early on, but we decided to head to the hospital at about 8 P.M. I grabbed my laptop so I could get a little work done over the next few days while she was in the hospital. After arriving at the hospital, it was determined that she would get an epidural so she could labor through the night while sleeping, so she got plenty of rest. "Cool," I thought, "I can lay on the couch in the room and sleep as well."

That did not happen! All I could think about as she fell asleep was my CRM. I had to build this thing out so I could do this whole "gorilla marketing" thing with my clients. I spent the whole night, probably 7 or 8 hours just building this thing out. I started by pulling a list of my clients and then categorizing them one-by-one as either an A, B, or C. I then built in an activity schedule for each of them individually based upon that rating. I determined to contact all A Clients four times each year: once for an annual review and the other three times just for a call to check in with them. For my B Clients it was a Review and one call to check in, and finally for my C Clients it would be just an Annual Review Card. I also built in birthday letters to go out a few days before each of their birthdays. "This is totally ingenious," I thought, and I was so excited! Heck, I think by the time Cyndi woke up and was about to go into delivering Sam I was more excited about having completed this project then I was for the delivery of my fourth child. I love Sam, and yes, I do love him more than my CRM, but that morning I was in a state of euphoria as I had my CRM built out and I had a beautiful baby boy!

Building out my CRM totally changed my business. I became a much better Financial Advisor, because now I was very intentional with staying in front of my clients. Hey, there is that critical word again, ___INTENTIONAL___. For the first time in my almost ten years of my career I started to receive unsolicited referrals. I believe the reason for this is because my clients noticed a change and also felt I was a better Advisor. People like to be appreciated, and our clients are no different. The more we reach out to them, the more it is obvious that we care about them and their accounts. Also, contacting them for an annual review is so important, and before I built out my CRM I had not been doing that. I was always just looking for the new sale with a new prospect. By reviewing each year, I got to know my clients much better and was really able to discover what was so important to them so that then I could help them achieve it.

From about 2008-2019, I used Redtail as my CRM. Since late in 2019 I have been using SalesForce. It is web-based, of course, and comes up with an app that I can access through my iPad and iPhone. It allows me to literally work from anywhere, and it allows me to not worry about how I can service my clients when I am unavailable or traveling. My assistant can utilize my CRM to keep us all organized and in tune with our clients.

I am sure most of you do use some sort of CRM. If you do not, it really is an absolute must if you are going to be successful in your business. I would encourage you to do some research and figure out what you need in your CRM and then purchase the one that best fits your needs. The best way to start your research is to just Google "CRM" within your industry. In our coaching work we were even able to help a pastor find one for his church.

It doesn't matter if you are a financial advisor or are in a totally different industry. If you work with clients or customers you should have a CRM. Even if you do non-profit work you should still be using a CRM to manage your donor database. The best source of a future donation is from an existing donor. The more you stay in front of them and reach out to them, the more likely they are to donate again. Ask other non-profits what they are using if you are unaware of this.

The important thing is to fully use your CRM. They can do so many different things to help you stay organized with your clients. You can create workflows for all service oriented items for your clients as well as for submitting and tracking new business. The feature I have always liked the most is the "Notes" section. Being able to input and track notes on any communication with clients is so important.

A lot of times when we get frustrated in business, it's because it seems like we always have more and more things to do. Your CRM can do so much for you and can truly keep you focused on your strengths. A lot of what you need to delegate can be delegated to your CRM. This allows you to automate so much of your business. Create the process to allow you to have more freedom, which will put you in your strengths zone.

If you don't have a CRM for your business, now is the time to put down this book and do a little research. Figure out which one might work best for you and your business. Once you determine which CRM is best for you, then be sure to be properly trained on what it can do for you. I know that even in my own business I am not fully utilizing my CRM. It takes time, but if you are intentional with the investment of your time then it will free you up to focus more on your strengths and do what you most enjoy.

Practice Ten: Staffing

"Maximize your strengths and
staff your weaknesses."[89]
John Maxwell

Back around 2008, one of the owners of the firm I worked for came to me shortly before Christmas and told me he had a tremendous Christmas gift for me. I asked him what it was, and he said, "Not what, but who!" He said that their former office manager, who after having children had at first decided to stay home, was now looking to work part time. He said she would be the perfect assistant for my dad and I. I asked a little about her and found out that she was a homeschool mom. I inquired even further, since Cyndi and I homeschooled our children. I found out that I had already known Deb and had actually worked with her as a staff member of some NCFCA Speech and Debate Tournaments. NCFCA is the National Christian Forensics and Communications Association, and our children com-

---

89 John Maxwell, *Today Matters* (New York, NY: Time Warner Book Group, 2004), p. 138.

peted in this league. I was very happy, since I knew how organized and skilled Deb was.

In preparation for our "interview" with Deb, I decided to put together some of the tasks that I felt I could delegate to someone else which would then free me up to meet with more clients. It was just a few things such as working with my CRM on all of the client tasks. The tasks mainly included making all of the phone calls to clients for either a review or just a check in call. I also included sending birthday letters as well as the Annual Review Statements we used to send out. My Dad and I figured we would need someone for about 12 hours per week to handle that work load for both of us. The reason I put "interview" in quotation marks is because it really wasn't an interview. I knew right away that I wanted to hire Deb because I already knew her, and from working with her at Speech and Debate Tournaments I knew what she was good at, and I knew she would be perfect to take on these tasks. I just showed her what we would need her to do and asked if it was something she would enjoy. She said she would, and so she started right after Christmas.

Deb was an absolute great hire, not just for my Dad and I, but for pretty much everyone in the office. Within a few short weeks it became very apparent that Deb could do in about 12 hours what most people do in about 20 hours per week. Once we figured this out we asked her to do some more, which now would include taking incoming client phone calls and helping them with simple service requests like a distribution from an account or a change of beneficiary. Deb was so talented that within about four years she was the leader of the entire Financial Services Team, managing six other Support Team Members while at the same time being my lead Account Manager for my clients. She was able to do all of this while usually working about 30 hours per week. She continued to increase her hours as her high-school aged kids got older and older. Deb is another reason why my practice really began to thrive. She was able to fill in for so many of my weaknesses. Not only was she very good at all of it, she was also passionate about it. She was clearly in her strengths zone. I was very blessed to work with her, and my clients were blessed by her as well.

Returning to the Maxwell quote: "Maximize your strengths and staff your weaknesses."[90] This is exactly what I was able to do with Deb. She filled in all of the gaps where I had gaps, and believe me there were many! She was able to perfectly complement my strengths with her own strengths. I always considered her and I, as well as the other Support Team Members of our team, as just that, a team. We needed each other to be the very best we could be. They did the things that I was not good at, and they did them extremely well. Working as a team led to great success.

Mother Teresa may have summed this all up best when she said, "I can do things you cannot; you can do things I cannot; together we can do great things."[91] Another great leader, Andrew Carnegie, said, "It marks a big step in your development when you come to realize that other people

[90] John Maxwell, *Today Matters*, (New York, NY: Time Warner Book Group, 2004) p 138

[91] , John Maxwell, *No Limits, Blow The Cap Off Your Capacity,* (New York, NY: Hachette Book Group, 2017), p. 294.

can help you do a better job than you can do alone."[92] John Maxwell is the one who shared those two quotes. He himself said, "If you want to multiply your effectiveness, you have to work with others."[93] I wish I would have discovered these three things many, many years before.

My lunch with Doug Pfeifer who advised me to utilize a CRM and my brief meeting with the former owner of my firm who encouraged me to hire Deb were the two greatest things that happened to my business. Now, I had my CRM keeping me organized and I also had a very small team to work with. I could do a much better job as a Financial Advisor. I became much, much more effective because I worked with others. As we added to the team, we tried to utilize each other's strengths to become the most effective team we could be.

Hiring staff can be very difficult to do, and I cannot say that I am an expert on hiring people. I love people, so almost everyone that comes into my office for an interview for a position seems to make the grade. I always just want to give the position to them. I try to always see the best in people, and because of that I could be in trouble and hire the wrong person. Thankfully, I have done a pretty good job of hiring support team members, but I have to admit that I think I have gotten pretty lucky. I have learned a lot about hiring staff from listening to podcasts and reading books. There are a whole lot of people out there who are experts on hiring, and that is why I turn to them.

It is better to be understaffed than to hire the wrong person quickly. Greg McKeown says, "If it isn't a clear yes,

---

[92] *Ibid.*, p. 294.
[93] *Ibid.*, p. 295.

then it's a clear no."[94] Also, he suggests that you ask yourself whether the prospective team member is someone you would like to work with every day. "If not," McKeown says, "then it is the wrong person."[95] There is no question that the team you assemble has to consists of members who are qualified for their work, and they also have to be good at what they do. However, in addition to being qualified, if they are not someone you would enjoy working with then it could be a disaster for your company culture. You want to enjoy coming to work each day, and therefore you should only hire people that you like.

Dave Ramsey gives 12 components to a good hire:

1. Prayer
2. Advertise and Get Referrals
3. The thirty minute drive-by interview
4. Résumé and References
5. Testing Tools like DISC Profile
6. Do You Like them and Do they Light Up
7. Personal Budget and Mission Statement
8. Compensation calculation
9. Benefits and Policy Review
10. Key Results Areas
11. Spousal interview
12. 90-day probation[96]

---

[94] Greg McKeown, *Essentialism*, (New York, NY: Crown Business, 2014), p. 109.

[95] *Ibid.,* p. 109.

[96] Ramsey, Dave, *Entreleadership* (New York, NY: Harper Books, 2011), pp, 135-147.

Now most of those 12 things involve gaining knowledge of the prospective hire. That is a lot to have to sort through, but Dave Ramsey has learned that hiring the wrong people can be quite costly. Not only can it be costly to your bottom line—because you have to fire someone and then rehire that position—it can also be costly to your company culture to hire the wrong person. I have not utilized all of the 12 items that Dave does, but I have definitely used some of them.

Another part of building a team is to do everything you can to help them grow and achieve their missions and visions in their lives and in their work. If the only reason you hire someone is to just take a load off of you, then you are not hiring for the right reason. You should be hiring someone to help you be more effective at what you do, but at the same time you should be helping them to be the most effective at what they can do. Zig Ziglar's most famous quote says, "You can have everything in life you want if you just help enough other people get what they want."[97] He further said, "When you see ability in others and then help nourish and develop that ability, you make some remarkable contributions."[98] We need to have the ability to see the potential in another person, and then persuade that person to use their ability.

Wow, just hiring people and building a team goes along with my own personal mission statement. I am all about serving others, and I should not just be serving my clients. If I follow Zig's lead then I should also be serving the team

---

[97] Zig, Ziglar, *See You At The Top* (Gretna, Louisiana: Pelican Publishing Co, 1982), p. 144
[98] *Ibid.*, p. 126.

members who work for me. It can be difficult to do this, but you must be intentional in investing in your team members. There is that word again: **intentional**.

Intentionality really is what it is all about when developing a team to work, not only for you, but *with you*. One of the things I have enjoyed most as a leader in my business is not only helping my clients but also helping my team leaders to become the very best at what they want to do. We hire people not so we can just sit around and be lazy, but we hire people to help us be better, and at that same time to help them grow.

The decision to leave my firm in 2018, after 12 years was extremely difficult. I was proud of the team that we had put together and that I was so blessed to work with. It was extremely difficult to walk away from them. As we had grown and become part of a larger company, the culture had changed. It was not quite what it once had been. It was still good, but I found it increasingly difficult within the new culture to be the best financial advisor I could be. The people there were good people, but I was at a crossroads. I wanted to best serve my clients, and I became convinced that I could do that best if I left that firm. I miss the team that I served with. If I could have brought them all along with me, I would, but it just wasn't possible. I knew when I started my new firm that I would have to work very hard to find new people to work with. They would have to help me to be the best financial advisor I could be. I would help them to fulfill what they wanted to get out of the work they were doing. It truly is a team effort.

If you are a team of one, then I want to encourage you to really think hard about where you are right now. Would you be able to better serve your clients, customers, or donors if you became a team of two? That may well be the case. Yes, it does cost money, but you should see it as *an investment* in the future. Remember you can best serve others if you focus on using your strengths. If there are things you are not good at that you are currently forced to do because you are a team of one, then you should be looking for someone who could handle those tasks more efficiently than you. They likely would be much more passionate about it than you are and could also do a much better job. In the long run, they could possibly even save you some money. Adding them would definitely allow you to produce more since you could dedicate more time to what you are good at.

So, now that you have hired an assistant or a team of people, it is important to know how to go about delegating things to other people. I have already touched upon delegation briefly in this chapter. However, I will go into much more detail in the chapter that follows. We were made to thrive. We can do that better within a team. Don't go it alone. Thrive together.

Practice Eleven: Delegation

want to start this chapter out by stating a truth that everyone ought to understand if they ever want to thrive in every area of their life. *We were not created to do absolutely everything because we are not capable of doing absolutely everything.* Even if we increased the amount of hours in a day and week, we would still not be able to do everything that we can think of. The bottom line is that we do not have enough time in each day to do everything, but even more importantly, we don't have the energy level to do absolutely everything.

One of the reasons I spent some time at the beginning of this book addressing our mission and vision along with our goals was to get us focused on what is truly important to us. I also wanted to focus and help you all understand the importance of putting together our perfect week. We should not go to our planner or calendar and put down what we are obligated to do first. No, we should actually put in our planner those things that are important to us. An example for me is putting in tasks to schedule in times with my kids, especially the older ones. I don't do this because I feel obligated as their father, but I do this because they are important to me, and I want to make sure that I give time to those things that are important to me.

Now the title of this chapter is "Delegation," and you may be wondering "Why is delegation so important?" Well, remember those things which are so important to us? Delegation is something we should be doing so that we can focus more on those things that are important to us. People get so caught up in the weeds of tasks, appointments, obligations, etc., that they often just simply forget what is most important to them. If certain tasks, appointments, etc., are delegated to someone at your office—specifically someone like a task manager or assistant-then you will have much more time to focus on what you love to do and what's most important to you. I realize that some of you may not have people that report to you, but I promise you there are things that you can delegate to someone else. Here is a simple example: we are having a dinner guest tonight, and when I got home, I knew that the dishwasher had to be emptied and dirty dishes in the sink had to go into the dishwasher. I started to do that, but then someone called who needed to talk to me and this was important and urgent. I asked my daughter to finish the chore I was working on. I delegated something that someone else could do so I could focus on the more important and urgent thing at that time.

It can be difficult to figure out what sorts of things you should be delegating. One of the reasons that I focused a whole chapter on strengths is so we can all understand that those tasks that we are good at and enjoy are typically not the types of things we should be delegating. We should be delegating those things that we are not good at or that we are not passionate about. Our old friend John Maxwell says, "Delegate so you are working smarter, not just harder. Do what you do best and drop the rest. Get control of your calendar; otherwise other people will. Do what you love because it will give you energy."[99] That pretty much sums up the art of delegation. You can only work so hard each day, so focus more on working smart. Also, focus on doing those tasks that give you energy, and delegate the rest. You will quickly find that you will be more free to operate within your strengths at work and will also have more time in the areas of your life that are important to you outside of work.

Maxwell goes on to say, "Stop doing important things **occasionally** and start doing important things **daily**."[100] The problem for most of us is that we usually choose to do those things that are urgent. Those urgent things are usually someone else's issue, and thus we put the important things on the back burner. Maxwell takes the opposite approach. The important things in life are those that should be done daily rather than occasionally.

We should be focusing all of our energy on those things that can lead us to be the very best at what it is God is calling us to do. Let me throw some truth into another myth. *God is not calling us to do everything.* If we try to do everything, then at best, we will do everything in only an average way. Actually, we will most likely be well below average. Greg McKeown says, "...only once you give yourself permission to stop trying to do it all, to stop saying yes to everyone,

[99] John Maxwell, *The 15 Invaluable Laws of Growth* (New York, NY: Hachette Book Group, 2012), p. 188.
[100] *Ibid.*, p. 236.

can you make your highest contribution towards the things that really matter."[101] He then defines Essentialism as less but better, meaning we should eliminate much of what we are doing so we can do those things that really matter in a much better way. He further says, "Essentialism is a disciplined, systematic approach for determining where our highest point of contribution lies, then making execution of those things almost effortless."[102] It should be where our full focus is.

McKeown then sums it all up by saying, "Essentialism is not about how to get more things done; it's about how to get the right things done."[103] As a Financial Advisor, something that is absolutely essential for me in my business is that I need to be the one meeting with clients, helping them with their planning, reviewing their investments and risk tolerance, and helping them determine what their objectives are. For me, in my business, those are the right things that I need to get done. Almost everything else can be delegated in some way. The appointment preparation, scheduling of the appointment, etc., I have delegated to my assistant. Also, do you want to know who can be the very best father to my children and spouse to Cyndi? Yep, you guessed it, that would be me. I need to spend more time doing the right thing for each of them. If that means I need to delegate the processing of some paperwork so I can attend a child's event then that is what I am going to do. I am the essen

---

[101] Greg McKeown, *Essentialism* (New York, NY: Crown Business, 2014), p. 5.
[102] *Ibid.,* p. 7.
[103] *Ibid.,* p. 5.

tial element of being a great father to my kids and husband to Cyndi.

Another way to look at all of this is the way Gary Keller and Jay Papasan ask, "What's the one thing you can do this week such that, by doing it, everything else would be easier or unnecessary?"[104] For these two authors, that is basically the starting point. Narrow it all down to one thing for the entire week. For me, in my business, that one thing is meeting with clients. As a father, that is spending time with my kids. For those two areas of my life, if I can get it down to that one thing, then everything else becomes easier or even unnecessary. Keller and Papasan also encourage us in their book to think every single day about what is the most important thing we need to do that day. We should then put that at the top of the list and put everything else aside until that one thing is accomplished. Heck, we can even delegate everything else that is not that one thing so all of our energy goes into that one thing. I use Michael Hyatt's Full Focus Planner, and for each day he has a daily big three. The concept is similar in that these are the three things that I absolutely must do on that day. Everything else is secondary and can either be put off or delegated. For me, I will try to delegate everything else.

So, how do I go about delegating? I follow the principles of McKeown, Keller & Papasan, and Hyatt. I start by focusing on those things that are important to me and that I am passionate about. I will do those things within that zone as well as those things that I am good at or are within

---

[104] Gary Keller & Jay Papasan, *The One Thing* (Austin, TX Bard Press, 2013), p. 9.

my strength zone. Brian Moran and Michael Lennington say, "You will need to guard your time intensely, delegating or eliminating everything possible that is not one of your strengths or does not help you advance your goals."[105] For these two authors it is all about doing the things that are within your strengths as well as those things that can help you to advance your goals. I will say that it is okay to delegate some things that help you advance your goals. I can tell you that providing good client service is very important for helping me to advance my business goals. A lot of this client service is delegated to others, however, so that I can focus more of my time in actual face-to-face meetings with my clients, because this is what I am very good at.

To take this even a step further, let me share with you what John Maxwell shares. He talks about focusing your energy. He suggests "...focusing on what is required of you that you have to do, on what will give you the best return by focusing on what you do well, and finally on what rewards you on what you love to do."[106] For Maxwell it is all about what is required of you that nobody else can do. Also, focus your efforts on what will give you the best return of your time based upon what are your strengths. It finally comes down to doing those things that rewards you personally as well as doing those things that you love to do. If I hated meeting with people one-on-one, then I would not be able to meet with my clients. I would have to delegate that to someone else and focus more on what else I may be good

---

[105] Brian P Moran & Michael Lennington, *The 12 Week Year* (Hoboken, NJ: John Wiley & Sons, Inc, 2013), p. 131.
[106] John Maxwell, *No Limits, Blow The Cap Off Your Capacity* (New York, NY: Hachette Book Group, 2017), p. 45.

at, such as, putting together the plan. I do enjoy putting together a plan for clients, but I also enjoy meeting with them. Doing both of these things energizes me.

Maxwell goes on further to say, "Stop doing what you are not great at doing."[107] Guilty as charged. Even though I am parading delegation in this chapter, I still fall into the "I need to and can do everything" syndrome. Even though I know better, I still at times do tasks that I am not even good at that someone else on my team is much better at. What is the impact on me? Well, doing things that I do not enjoy and are not within my own personal strengths drains me of my energy. It also takes time away from those things that I am really good at and gets me going. I imagine that when you read that you must think I am an idiot when I do that. Well, you are right; I am! To make it worse, the people I would delegate those other tasks to could do it better than me, and it would actually energize them because it is something they are passionate about. Honestly, delegation is great and betters everyone involved, the delegator as well as those who are being delegated to!

Maxwell also talks about the importance of working with a team of people. It is just impossible to achieve your objectives on your own, especially if you have a huge vision. By putting together a team, they can help you to grow as you invest in them to help them achieve what they want to do. You can also help them to focus on doing what they are good and passionate about. If you assign them tasks that are within those two zones for them, then they will truly flourish.

---

[107] *Ibid.*, p. 145.

Maxwell quotes the great Brian Tracy. Tracy said, "Successful men and women are those who work almost all the time on high value tasks."[108] I would say those high value tasks are those tasks that are within their strength and passion zone. So, if you focus on those tasks that are within those two zones and you delegate to your team members tasks that are also within their strengths and passion zones, then you and your team will be running on all cylinders in the most efficient and productive way.

In this chapter I want to make sure I provide you with actual applications to use in deciding the best tasks to delegate, as well as figuring out who to delegate those tasks to. In order to do this, I want to go back to Michael Hyatt. I cannot emphasize to you enough the importance of taking his course, but I do want to give you a few high level ideas from his course to help you with this. Trust me when I say that my summary of his ideas is not enough. You have to enroll in his class if you truly want it to change your life. For now, here are some of his thoughts and ideas on delegation.

From: Free To Focus Course[109]

In Lesson Four of his course, Micheal Hyatt suggests that before you can determine what to delegate you need to create a *not to do* list. These are items that you are neither passionate at nor proficient in.

---

[108] *Ibid.,* p. 218.
[109] Michael Hyatt, *Free To Focus*, https://freetofocus.com

You might think that in order to delegate, an assistant is definitely required and recommended. However, this is not necessarily the case. Hyatt also makes very clear that you don't need to hire an assistant to begin delegating now. In Lesson Five he provides ideas on how to accelerate your productivity by automating repetitive tasks. He says to look at opportunities for self-automation, such as having a morning routine and end-of-the-day routine. One idea of how automation works is template automation. Template automation can be something as simple as using different email templates. These would be common email responses that you can use to respond to clients and vendors. He also provides a process automation by using workflows. These define how you do a particular job or task. In putting together a workflow you will document every step you take with the task. Do not leave anything out. By writing down how particular tasks can be done it is a great reminder for you on how to do things but also to be able to more easily train someone to whom you can delegate these tasks. You may also be able to build workflows into your CRM and then automate certain tasks within the CRM. In essence, by doing this you are delegating something to a program rather than a person. I do this with my birthday greetings that I send out each year to clients.

In Lesson Six, Hyatt gives five levels of delegation: Level one is: "Do exactly what I've asked you to do." Level two is: "Research the topic and report back to me." Level three is: "Research the topic, outline the options, and make a recommendation." Level four is: "Make a decision, and then tell me what you did." Level five is: "Make whatever decision you think is best."

I think it is critical to really understand these five different levels of delegation. I mentioned my assistant Deb in a previous chapter. During the last few years that I worked with her I was able to use Level Five Delegation with her. There may have been some tasks where I would use Level Three or Four but for the most part they were Level Five. I had grown to trust her to make the right decision on most things. Sometimes I just wanted her to follow up with me, and other times I just really wanted her to work through the details and then give me a suggestion on what she thought was best.

It takes time to get comfortable enough with someone to give someone Level Five Delegation. It has to be someone you like and have worked with for a while. Even with that person, much like it was for me with Deb, there may be tasks that you don't delegate at that high of a level. When you first start working with someone you will likely be using Level One and Two with most tasks, at least until you can see that they are strong in many areas that you need.

A critical aspect of delegation, whether that is to a person or a CRM, is to decide the appropriate person or CRM where you delegate each task. If you are delegating certain tasks to a certain person, then make sure you try to delegate those tasks that they are both passionate and proficient with. Finally, once you have delegated, it is important to communicate verbally as well as to provide them with a copy of the workflow, which you should have already created.

Some people refer to Work Flows as Standard Operating Procedures or SOP's. I have chosen to refer to them as Work Flows because I learned that term by taking Michael Hyatt's Courses and listening to his podcasts. I find his verbiage helpful. As a way to provide you with further application ideas I thought I would share with you some of my Work Flows. I am constantly reviewing these and creating new ones based upon what the needs are for my firm so we can provide the best experience for our clients. Here are a few I will share:

Posting To LinkedIn

1. This process is done every two weeks on a Monday or Tuesday.
2. Go to buffer.com to login.
   a. Click on the login link in the upper right hand corner.
   b. Login through LinkedIn. Username is tojeda@ xxxx.com and Password is XXXXXX
   c. The page to post content will show up.
3. Go to platinumstrategies.com and login by hitting the login link in the top middle of the page.
   a. Login with XXXXX as the Username and XXXXX as the password.
   b. With your mouse, hover over the Communications tab towards the top. Scroll to Weekly Emails and click.
   c. Click on the most recent Weekly Update. Then on the next page you have the option to open

     it up as a Word Document, proceed with this option.

   d. Once in that document go to the last page where there are hyperlinks.

4. Copy a hyperlink of an article and then go to the Buffer website and paste the link into the What Do You Want to Share Link. Sometimes the first few hyperlinks are not actual articles, but rather graphs. It is important to only copy and paste actual articles.

5. Once a highlight of that article pops up then schedule the post by clicking on the arrow to the Right of "Add to Queue."

6. Click on Schedule Post.

7. Only post items on Monday through Friday (not on Saturday or Sunday). In scheduling the post do so for the next available day from the last post. Schedule the time for anywhere between 9 AM and 11 AM.

8. Repeat steps 4 through 7 until all 10 posts are filled for the next two weeks.

Appointment Preparation

1. Review Calendar for upcoming week to see what appointments are coming up.

2. For Individual Appointments

   a. Determine what kind of accounts the client has by reviewing Albridge on Producer Workbench for Ameritas, Redtail, and other areas to see where a client may have money. Be sure to have all information. Some accounts or life policies may not show up on Albridge. This would include Global Atlantic Variable Annuities, American Equity, Voya and others.

b. Put together Agenda which would include, What's New?, Review of IRA's if any, Review of Non Qualified Accounts if any, Review of Life Insurance if any, Savings, Estate Planning, Additional Needs, and Email Update.

c. Review Redtail Notes from previous meetings. It may mean to review notes from the previous two to three years or even several years before that.

    i. Note any items that should be discussed in the Review Meeting. Are there any notes pertaining to them retiring soon, notes about their other investments or Retirement Accounts through work? Are there notes where Tony or Rene' had made suggestions that were not followed through on, maybe allocation change, or a new investment or insurance ideas? If there are any of these items then copy and paste that particular note along with the date of the note to be included in the folder. Highlight the specifics and also make a notation in the Calendar for that client meeting.

    ii. Provide any further instructions to Tony on items that maybe he should be discussing in the review meeting based upon the review of the notes.

d. In Client Meeting Folder include the following if needed:

i. Agenda

ii. Albridge Report if there is one.

iii. Most Recent Statement for any Life Policies

iv. GLWB Information for any Variable Annuities or Index Annuities

v. Note interest rate of any Fixed Annuities or the Fixed Account in a Variable Annuity.

vi. Investor Questionnaire

Service Paperwork Submission

1. Tony emails the Service Paperwork to Assistant through a Secure Email.
2. Assistant puts documents into Redtail Imaging
3. Assistant searches for the client name.
4. Assistant then clicks on the appropriate account file that pertains to that client account.
5. Assistant then uploads the document into this folder. Do this by clicking on the folder icon with a downward arrow toward the upper right hand corner. Then click on the Upload Image tab.

1. Either drag and drop the image or hit the select tab. If hitting the select tab then select the document to be imaged. Then hit the green upload button.

6. For Ameritas paperwork submission:
   7. Assistant logs into Ameritas' Producer Workbench.
   8. Under the Ameritas logo they click on her name and then click on the messages tab.
   9. If submitting paperwork for an annuity:
      1. Under the New Message heading click on the Annuity NB/Service tab and follow instructions.
   2. If submitting paperwork for a Life or DI Policy:
      3. Under the New Message heading click on the Life/DI/VUL Service tab and follow instructions.
   4. If submitting paperwork for AIC Account such as NFS Account:
      5. Under the New Message heading click on the AIC Document Submission tab and follow instructions.

I am sure that these workflows mean nothing to you, but they are very, very meaningful to me. They not only explain the process to my team, they also remind me about how I best perform certain tasks. Why is it important for me to have these documented for myself? If I lose team members, I may need to have to do some of these tasks temporarily myself. The important thing to remember is that, because they are documented, you are able to easily train someone else how to do it.

Overall in my practice, I have several workflows. I will review these workflows with my team every so often to see if they need to be updated or even removed. We are also always looking to create new ones so we can make sure everyone is on the same page.

The important thing for you is to be very clearly thinking about what are the items that you need done that would be best delegated to someone else. Then think through what are all of the action steps that need to be taken to complete the task. Then write them down. It is that simple, and then it is simple to duplicate in the future. I want to encourage you to take some time in the next day or two to begin putting together some workflows for yourself and your team. Be sure to be very specific and clear in what you put down. Once you have them written down then review them with each team member who will be doing that particular task.

We were made to thrive, but it takes a team to truly thrive. Work together to be as productive and efficient as you can possibly be. You can do this! It is a big step and something you should do now. Even if you don't have a team of people yet, it would still be a great idea to put together some workflows anyway. Go get started.

Wow, you have done such a great job so far in this book. The very last section will cover two areas that I think can really take you to the top in your career. These two ideas will separate you from the rest.

Tips For Taking You To The Top

Practice Twelve: Thank You's:
An Attitude Of Gratitude

What are you thankful for? No really. That's not a rhetorical question. What are you truly grateful for? This is a question we should be asking of ourselves regularly and by regularly, I don't just mean once a year on Thanksgiving. We ought to be asking ourselves this question every day! To be completely honest, I have not always done this, and if I have, I rarely have done it very well. In fact, I would say that more often than not I am complaining. That's right, the author of a book entitled "Made2Thrive" has struggles with complaining!

Let's be honest, no one likes a complainer, and complaining clearly does nothing good for anyone. Have you ever heard someone say about a chronic complainer, "Man, that complainer is a standup person! They must be really thriving in their life!" No! You simply don't hear that. Even though I've had my fair share of struggles with complaining in the past, over the past few years I have been trying much harder to be grateful. However, it takes work. Being grateful isn't a one-time decision and BOOM! You're instantly grateful all of the time. Being grateful is a choice. A daily choice. Sometimes even a small choice. We can choose to be grateful or we can choose to be a complainer.

One of the things that I have tried to do over the past couple of years to help me be a more grateful person is to take some time in silence and think about all those things that I have been blessed with in my life. I find that doing this either during my morning prayer time or in a Holy Hour is the best time for me. I have been truly blessed in my life and so I take the time to reflect on all of these blessings and then to thank God for everything He has done for me.

Here are just some of the things I am thankful for:

1. Cyndi and my relationship with her. I have been blessed in marriage since June 11, 1994 and 4.5 years before that was when we met. She is such a giving person and is always trying to make others and me happy.

2. My six children here on this earth, as well as the two children we lost in miscarriage. The six on this earth really give me so much joy. I am proud to be their father and love watching them grow into the strong leaders that they are. They each have their own unique gifts, and I love watching them use them. I am also very grateful for the two little precious souls I have in heaven. I love the 4th commandment, "Honor Your Father and Mother." I know that my two little saints in heaven are praying for Cyndi, myself, and their six siblings.

3. I am blessed with two wonderful parents, two great siblings, and my in-laws. I love spending time with my extended family.

4. I am blessed to have such a wonderful career. Each day that I go to work I get to do something I am passionate about: helping my clients achieve their dreams and desires.

5. I have some of the greatest friends a man could ever have. I love to spend time with them, help them when they are in need, and I also know they will always help me when I am in need.

6. My faith is a tremendous blessing to me. Yes, I sometimes reject God, but I know He is an ever merciful Father. I love to spend time in prayer and meditation.

That is just part of what I am thankful for. I am thankful for so much more, and every time I spend time in quiet thinking of each blessing I thank God for giving me those blessings. This is how I practice a spirit of gratitude. Brian Buffini encourages people to write down or to even say out loud those things they are thankful for. I agree with him when he affirms that gratitude is transformational and has the power to change your thinking from scarcity to abundance. Buffini quotes Cicero, "Gratitude is not only the greatest of your virtues, but the parent of all others."[110] This basically means that it is quite difficult to practice the other virtues if we are not first practicing gratitude.

---

[110] Brian Buffini, *The Emigrant Edge*, (New York, NY: Howard Books, 2017), p. 129.

Buffini suggests that we appreciate those closest to us. What is a great way to do that? Have you ever noticed with your children how many times we nag them compared to how often we praise them? I would suggest trying to reverse that order. Praise them many more times than you nag them. Point out all of the times you see them doing something good. Do this not only with your children, but do it with your team at work and friends as well. Gratitude is great for you and everyone you associate with. Being grateful and recognizing your blessings daily is a great way to live your life. If you want to live a good life then practice being grateful for your blessings.

When I first started my career it was very common for me to send out letters thanking people for meeting with me or thanking them for their business. That was great, but it was mostly a form letter with maybe a unique sentence to that particular client. Brian Buffini teaches his clients to write personal notes to your clients, co-workers, family, and friends. After I read his book and started listening to his podcasts I started doing the same thing. I strive to send out hand written cards each week. It is much more personable and the people that I send them to genuinely appreciate them. It leaves a positive impression on them and it also helps to lift them up, especially if they are having a bad day when they receive it.

I had sent an individual a card when I heard that they recently had a minor surgery. This person was not a client of mine and not even a close friend. The next time I saw her at a dinner event she came up to me and thanked me for the card. I have had that happen quite a few times in the past couple of years.

Michael Hyatt also weighs in on gratitude. He shares with us that gratitude can boost our resiliency "because it keeps us hopeful, reminds us we have agency, improves our patience, and expands possible responses. It keeps us hopeful because gratitude keeps us positive and optimistic..."[111] Now that's what I am talking about. Positivity and being optimistic are so much better than being negative all of the time. I will also say that when we have an attitude of gratitude we are just a happier person. When we have this attitude of thankfulness people will also want to be around us. We are like a magnet for others. Hyatt also says in regard to our possible responses, "Gratitude moves us into a place of abundance, a place where we're more resourceful, creative, generous, optimistic, and kind."[112] "Gratitude has the potential to amplify everything good in our lives. It is the best remedy I know for the affliction of scarcity thinking and the best way to cultivate a mindset of abundance."[113]

Why would we not want to have each of those qualities and traits? I know full well what Hyatt is referring to when he talks about this idea that gratitude amplifies everything good in our lives. When I am a very thankful person I see the good in others much more clearly. That way even when one of my children may be having a bad day of listening, I still see so much good in them. Whereas, if I just always had

---

[111] Michael Hyatt, *Your Best Year Ever*, (Grand Rapids, MI: Baker Books, 2018), p. 91.
[112] *Ibid.,* p. 92.
[113] *Ibid.,* p. 93.

a negative attitude, I promise you that when they are having a bad day I would only see what is wrong with them.

There are a whole lot of ways to practice gratitude, and I have covered some ideas of what I personally do. I have heard Jon Gordon talk about taking a thankfulness walk. This is maybe when you are having a bad day and have a bad attitude and so you just go on a walk and think of those things that you should be thankful for. I also know others who start their prayer time in much the same way that I do and focus on the blessings that God has given to them. Many people keep a gratitude journal. I do not do that, but I have used my journal as part of my gratitude in my prayer time.

The more we practice being thankful, the more others will be drawn to us. The more others are drawn to us, the better it is for our business and our personal life. Would it not be true that all of us could expand our businesses if we just had more customers who did business with us? Well, if you are a thankful person then this will automatically begin to happen. Who should you be sending a thank you to today? Maybe make a list of some people and spend 30 minutes working on some cards. I promise that if you take the time to do this today and then form it as a daily or weekly habit, it will change your business life as well as your personal life.

When you practice gratitude, more people will be attracted to you, and then you will find that it is easier to be referable. The next chapter is on this very important topic which really leads to success in business.

Practice Thirteen: Be Referable

M any years ago, when I was very new in my career as a Financial Advisor, I attended the NAIFA Lincoln Association Luncheon to listen to Bill Cates. Bill was known as the Referral Coach, and he was an expert on helping those in my industry as well as other industries to get more referrals. Of course, since I was only in about the second year of my career, I had already gone through all of my friends and family members and now I needed to find a better way to get in front of more people. Cold Calling was an absolute disaster for me, and so I was excited to listen to Bill's presentation.

At that Luncheon, I picked up on some really good tips and tricks! Bill gave many ideas on how to go about asking for referrals. His ideas were very helpful, and I was excited to begin utilizing some of his suggestions. I also remember that he had a book for sale that day and I bought it and promptly devoured it! I was eager to learn! That book was probably the first book in regard to a business that I ever read. There was one thing that stood out about his presentation, as well as within his book. It was the idea that we have to become referable. I was very happy that in both his presentation and in his book he went over what it meant to "be referable". To summarize Cates points, you want to be so good at what you do that people just have a desire to refer others to you without you even asking. Basically, be exceptional in the work that you do and referrals will just come!

I have written in this book about the journey of success. I have talked about what it takes to thrive. In business you can truly thrive if you are able to obtain <u>unsolicited referrals.</u> I knew that I had to become the very best Advisor that I could be in order for others to feel comfortable enough to just give my name out to others. I did not want to have to ask people for referrals because I knew in my own experience how awkward and uncomfortable that is. Thankfully, after about the first 15 years of my career I had become referable. Take note of that—15 years! Yes, even becoming referable is about the journey. One does not simply become referable overnight; it takes time to build your business and grow professionally before you become referable. It takes work. It's about the journey!

Since that point I have averaged about 2 referrals per month. I realize that this is a very small number for those of you who are really good at asking for and getting referrals, but for me it is a great number. I did not have to ask for these referrals. In fact clients will often ask me if I am taking new clients because they may have someone that needs to meet with me. Then, about a week or so later I get a call from that friend. I have found that unsolicited referrals are golden. I would estimate that 90% of those become my clients. This is a much, much better percentage than I used to get when I was asking people for a list of names. The reason for this is the fact that they are already interested in working with me as opposed to me pursuing and wanting to work with people who probably are not interested in the first place. Building up your business and becoming incredibly proficient in what you do is a much better strategy than simply reaching out and asking for referrals. Become referable; don't look for referrals.

Brian Buffini says, "Become exceptional. When you're exceptional, people talk about you. When you're exceptional, you're likely to get promoted. When you're exceptional, your clients refer you to other customers."[114] It takes an extraordinary effort to become exceptional. It is important to follow all of the other steps that I have outlined in this book to help you become exceptional. Put together your mission statement. Have a vision for where you want to be. Take action by putting together goals to help you achieve your vision. Be accountable and work within your strengths. Utilize a CRM and learn to delegate to others. Also, always have an attitude of gratitude. By following these steps you will be working to become exceptional.

Buffini goes on to say, "Make your customers feel valued.[115] "Go the extra mile."[116] "This means making more effort than is expected of you. Create meaningful relationships with your clients by treating them as kings and queens."[117] This is very helpful advice as well.

---

[114] Brian Buffini, *The Emigrant Edge*, (New York, NY: Howard Books, 2017), pp. 216-217.
[115] *Ibid.*, p. 217.
[116] *Ibid.*, p. 223.
[117] *Ibid.*, p. 231.

I do realize that I fail sometimes to make my customers feel valued. It is something I need to do a much better job at. When customers leave, which is not very often, it usually comes down to them not feeling valued, and that is totally my own fault. In my firm, I try to help each individual with a very customized plan. My suggestions on how they should invest are based entirely on what they want out of life and how much they are willing to risk. I want to help them achieve their dreams and goals, and therefore I do not have an off-the-shelf solution for everyone. My suggestions are for them and are very specific to them. We also reach out to our clients anywhere from 1 to 4 times a year. Several of these outreaches are just to check in with them, but at least once a year we are reaching out to them to ask them to review. Some choose not to review each year, but we always give them the opportunity to and remind them of the importance of an annual review. Once someone becomes a client at our business, I have come to know and understand how critical it is to be intentional. I really do care about my clients, and I want them to know that based on how well I treat them—not only when they come in for an appointment, but all throughout the year.

Buffini also suggests the idea of welcoming your clients' suggestions on what you can improve. I have done this several different ways in my career. I have sent them a survey to complete. I have asked them in their annual reviews. I have also had groups of clients come in for Focus Group Lunches for the specific purpose of finding out what they thought we could do better. The important thing about asking for suggestions is that you have to be willing to act upon them.

I have always tried to do this and if for some reason they gave a suggestion that I would not act on I would always let them know why we chose not to.

When I first started my career my Dad told me to always do what is in the best interest of my prospect or client. He told me to never worry about what commission I would earn, and that if I always did what was best for my client then I would be successful for a long time to come. He finally said that there are many who get into our business and may be successful for a few short years. Those are usually the ones who are doing everything they can to earn the highest commissions and not being concerned about what was in the best interest of the client. I have tried to live those principles not just in my business but in every area of my life.

Being referable is important whether you are a Financial Advisor or in any other career field. The easiest way to bring in new business is through referrals. If you work at a hospital and the care you provide is exceptional, then it will lead to others talking about the hospital in a very favorable way. Just take a look at Facebook in the next few days. I am sure you will find at least one person asking for a recommendation of something. People will then post tons of comments about who they are referring and why. Are you kidding me? Word of mouth is the very best advertisement.

Even if you are in the non-profit world, it is important to be referable. If your organization does a tremendous job of fulfilling a need in the community, then you are likely to get bigger and better donations from more people. So, regardless of what field you are in, it is so important to serve others and to serve them well. People will talk about you in a favorable way and that will lead to more referrals.

Ultimately, if we want to be referable and remain that way, then we need to be consistent in being exceptional as well as providing value to our clients. If we provide the highest quality care and service to our clients, then they will show their appreciation by doing future business with us and by referring their friends to us as well. Be the best at what you do and others will talk about you and promote you to others. Be referable!! You were made to thrive. Do so by serving others.

Conclusion

Remember when you first started reading this book? Early on, I discussed success as being much more about the **journey** rather than the destination. We can always be getting better. We can always be moving forward. As we move forward we become successful as a result of the journey that we are on. It is when we are not moving forward that we become stagnant, and therefore we are not successful. Stagnation is the enemy of the successful. I would encourage all of you reading this book to strive for success. Take each day and win each day. Get better each day and get closer to your life vision.

I have tried to lay out in this book some steps that we can all take to truly thrive in this world. I want to encourage all of you to read through this book again (that's right, again), and take the actions necessary to thrive. Don't just sit there! Take action now!

As a way to conclude this book, I want to review the steps I have covered so that we can all truly thrive in this world.

The first step was to **create a mission statement**. A mission statement explains the *why* of what you do. It should direct everything you do in life, every choice you make, every action you do. A mission statement keeps you focused on doing what you are gifted at and passionate about.

I next suggested that you **come up with some sort of a life vision.** A vision is where you want to be sometime in the future. It is not a short term vision, but more of a longer term vision. The actions and steps you take in life should assist you in achieving your long term vision. You won't always do this perfectly, but if the tasks we do each day bring us closer to our vision then we will be much happier in life and also we will be successful.

I then suggested **putting together goals** that will help you to achieve your long term vision. These are not the action steps for us, but are rather things we want to achieve in the next three to 12 months which will then get us closer to our vision. There are a whole lot of different types of goals that we can set up. These goals should cover all of the different areas of our life which we see in our future longer term vision. Achieving the goals will help to give us the momentum to actually achieve the longer term vision.

I discussed the importance of **Action Steps.** These are the next best steps that you can take each and every day to help you get closer to your goals, and ultimately your Life Vision. Review your goals and Vision each week so you can come up with new action steps for the next days and weeks.

I have also laid out **the importance of accountability.** I think it is vitally important to share your longer term vision along with your goals with a select group of people. This could be your spouse, close friends, co-workers, coach, or manager. It has to be someone who is willing to really challenge you and to find out why you are not progressing forward if you are struggling. It also has to be a person who will provide you with the encouragement you need to keep moving forward.

Coaching is also a very important aspect of Made2Thrive. Coaches motivate us to achieve our goals. They also hold us accountable to the things we said we were going to do. They also can assist us in coming up with new action steps to move us closer to our goals. I cannot emphasize enough the importance of coaching. If you would like to visit with us about what we offer then please email us at thrive@made2thrive.live. You can also review the options on our website Made2Thrive.live.

I also spent an entire chapter on trying to **come up with your perfect week.** This is going to be different for everyone and should be dictated by what is important to you. How do you know what is important to you? You have already done it by laying out your mission, life vision, and goals. Now, lay out a week that reflects all of that.

In the next step I discussed the importance of **working within our strengths.** The bottom line is that if we are trying to do everything on our own and spend too much time in an area of weakness then we will struggle to achieve our goals or our long term vision. We cannot do everything on our own. We have to focus on working mostly within the areas that we are strongest.

I then focused on two areas that will help us to stay within our strengths zone. These were **utilizing a Client Relationship Management system** as well as **delegating to others**. A CRM is meant to help you in assisting your clients and at the same time a tool to help steer your business. Much of what is done within a CRM is automated, and the more things we can automate the more effectively we are able to stay within our strengths zone. Also, delegating tasks and services that we are not as strong in will allow us to focus on what we are truly good at.

The next step I covered was **having a strong sense of gratitude.** Be grateful with everything you have been blessed with. It only takes a few minutes a day to really reflect how you have been blessed. By doing this you will feel much more positive about everything you are doing. Also, it is important to express that gratitude to others. Be sure to share your gratefulness with your spouse, children, friends, co-workers, and clients.

Finally, I addressed **being referable.** If you take all of the other steps I have laid out in this book, then becoming referable will happen naturally. Be the best at whatever you are doing. Truly strive to thrive in serving others, and people will want to introduce you to others. This isn't just in business. If you do a great job of serving others in the other areas of your life, then you will get introduced to a whole lot of people.

I believe we were made to thrive. The more everyone in our world strives to be the very best they can be then the better off our whole world will be. If we want to live in a better world, then it starts with us becoming the very best we can be at whatever our mission in life is. Get out there and thrive!!!

Acknowledgements

I have so many people to thank for the assistance of this book. I must first thank my Heavenly Father for inspiring me to actually write it. I also need to thank my son, Andrew, who encouraged me to begin Made2Thrive as a Division of Integrity Center. I enjoy working with him each day and am excited to see how much more we can serve by coaching individuals to help and make them thrive. Andrew was also very instrumental in helping to provide many revisions to this book, and none of it would have been possible without his help.

I want to thank Cyndi for being the very best wife a man can have. She is so supportive of me and all of the crazy ideas I come up with. Without her support I would not be able to fulfill my mission each day. I want to thank my daughter, Rachel, for all of her help with our Made2Thrive Workshop and Workbook. I don't have the talent to put something like that together and am very grateful for her assistance. I also want to thank Lindsay, Sam, and Emma for believing in me and putting together your own Mission Statement, Vision, Goals, and Action Steps. Thank you also to my youngest, Joseph. You always bring a smile to my face. Go Yankees!!

Thank you to all of you for taking the time to read this book. I hope it will help you to thrive in your life.

About The Author

Tony Ojeda is married to his beautiful wife, Cyndi. They have six children. He is blessed by his family and loves to spend time with each one of them. Tony began his career in the Financial Services Industry as an Insurance Agent and Registered Representative in 1994. He has been a Certified Retirement Counselor for many years. He began coaching individuals on their journey to success when he was the Managing Partner of a former firm. In 2018 he sold his stock and bought back most of his book of business and started his own firm, Integrity Center. In 2020 he created a new Division called Made2Thrive offering workshops and coaching to help leaders thrive in their own six life domains.

Would You Want To Work With Us

We would be more than happy to help you on your journey of success. We offer day-long workshops for companies to begin the process of assisting leaders to begin thriving in their lives. We also offer one-on-one coaching to help individuals really move the needle on their journey of success and to truly help in living out their mission each day. If you are looking for a keynote speaker on anything from Living Your Mission to a Life-Long Vision or more then please reach out to us as well.

Our website is Made2Thrive.live. Please check us out. You can also contact us by emailing us at thrive@made2thrive.live

Bibliography

Buffini, Brian *The Emigrant Edge*, (New York, NY: Howard Books, 2017)

Hill, Napoleon, *Think and Grow Rich The Landmark Bestseller Now Revised And Updated For the 21ST Century*, (New York, NY: Penguin Group, 2005)

Hyatt, Michael, *Free To Focus*, https://freetofocus.com

Hyatt, Michael, *Your Best Year Ever*, (Grand Rapids, MI: Baker Books, 2018)

Keller, Gary & Papasan, Jay, *The One Thing*, (Austin, TX: Bard Press, 2013)

Maxwell, John, *3 Things Successful People Do*, (Nashville, TN: Nelson Books, 2016)

Maxwell, John *Failing Forward*, (Nashville, TN: Thomas Nelson, Inc, 2000)

Maxwell, John, *Intentional Living*, (New York, NY: Hachette Book Group, 2017)

Maxwell, John, *No Limits, Blow The Cap Off Your Capacity*, (New York, NY: Hachette Book Group, 2017)

Maxwell, John, *The 15 Invaluable Laws of Growth*, (New York, NY: Hachette Book Group, 2012)

Maxwell, John, *Today Matters*, (New York, NY: Time Warner Book Group, 2004)

McKeown, Greg, *Essentialism*, (New York, NY: Crown Business, 2014)

Moran, Brian P. & Lennington, Michael, *The 12 Week Year*, (Hoboken, NJ: John Wiley & Sons, Inc, 2013)

Nightingale, Earl, "Success: a worthy destination - Nightingale-Conant."
http://www.nightingale.com/articles/success-a-worthy-destination/

Ramsey, Dave, *Entreleadership*, (New York, NY: Harper Books, 2011)

Sinek, Simon, *Start With Why,* (New York, NY: Penguin Group, 2009)

Tracy, Brian, "The Power of Habit: 7 Steps to Successful Habits https://www.
briantracy.com/success/personal/op/the-power-of-habit.html.

Vaden, Rory, *Take The Stairs,* (New York, NY: Penguin Group, Inc, 2012)

Ziglar, Zig, *See You At The Top*, (Gretna, Louisiana: Pelican Publishing
Co, 1982)